Old-Fashioned Cookies

Favorite Cookie
Recipes That
Bring Back
Warm Memories
of Childhood

Old-Fashioned Cookies

1st Printing   January 2005
2nd Printing   February 2006
3rd Printing   March 2006
4rd Printing   July 2006

ISBN 1-931294-47-X - Hardcover
ISBN 1-931294-55-0 - Paperback

Library of Congress Number: 2004116142

Illustrations by Nancy Murphy Griffith

Edited, Designed and Published in the
United States of America
Printed in the U.S.A.
Cookbook Resources, LLC
541 Doubletree Drive
Highland Village, Texas 75077
Toll free 866-229-2665
www.cookbookresources.com

Introduction

Do you have a sweet cookie memory? Ever counted the chocolate chips, made criss-cross designs with a fork, raided the refrigerator for a pinch of icebox cookie dough, rolled Snickerdoodles in cinnamon and sugar or decorated cut-outs with icing and sprinkles?

Hot, homemade, fresh-from-the-oven cookies are as universal as, well ... cookies! But their long and sweet history dates back to the ancient kingdom of Persia, one of the first countries to grow sugarcane.

Derived from the Dutch word koekje, meaning "little cake," the cookie as we know it made its first appearance quite by accident, as a bit of cake batter cooked to test oven temperature. The individual-size cake caught on, and cookie recipes are found in most every country and culture around the world today.

English, Scotch and Dutch settlers brought cookies to colonial America in the form of "tea cakes" (mild, flat cookies flavored with butter) and "Snickerdoodles" (dough rolled in cinnamon before baking). Despite their early introduction, cookies did not become popular with Americans until the early 20th century. The accidental invention of the chocolate chip cookie in 1930 sparked the first real "cookie craze" in the U.S., when the Nestle Semi-Sweet Chocolate Company partnered with the cookie's inventor Ruth Wakefield to market the new treat.

Early American cookies were sweetened with molasses, before refined sugar became readily available. Sugar rationing during World War II only briefly slowed the cookie's evolution, and post-war America embraced the cookie in its many forms. Food companies like Nestle®, Quaker®, Skippy® and Kellogg's® played a big role in establishing the cookie as its own "food group." They printed cookie recipes on their packaging and promoted now-famous cookie ingredients like chocolate chips, oatmeal, peanut butter and cereal.

Today the chocolate chip cookie is the most popular cookie in the United States and Canada, and the pre-packaged cookie market generates over $6 billion annually. Cookie recipes, ingredients and high-tech "gadgets" - all in the name of the "perfect" cookie – abound.

Though ready-to-bake and ready-to-eat cookies are widely available, modern cooks still make these versatile sweets "from scratch," ensuring that our children will always know what it's like to enjoy warm cookies and conversation.

Who'd have guessed that a simple spoonful of cake batter would become the stuff memories (and popular culture) are made of? As you browse these recipes, old and new, I hope you'll make your own memories with those you love.

Contents

*Here's one great cookie dough you can keep in the
refrigerator or freezer. When you want homemade cookies
in a hurry, just pull out the cookie dough, add a few
ingredients and heat up the oven. Hot homemade cookies in
minutes!*

*Make the dough, form into lots of little balls, flatten a little and stick
a thumb in them. Literally, that's where thumbprint cookies get their
name. In each little indentation, they hold a special treat.*

*Roll out the cookie dough into several layers, add
some goodies on top and roll them together into a
log. Slice into small pieces and bake away. You'll
love the results.*

*Make some cookies and put them together with a
special center of sweet, gooey goodness. It's the best kind of sandwich.*

*Get a big spoon of dough and drop the dough on a baking sheet. No
special treatment for this dough, but the taste is plenty special.
Chocolatey Chocolate, Peanutty Peanut Butter, Chewies, Crunchies,
Crispies, Fruit, Macaroons, Butterscotch, Shortbreads, Sugar,
Oatmeal and Gum-Drop Cookies*

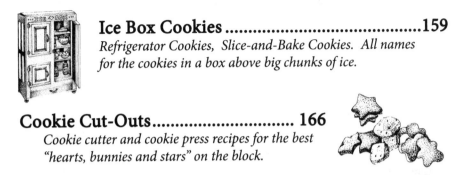

Basic Cookie Dough

*This basic cookie dough can be made any time and chilled
or frozen to use later. Recipes on pages 7-11 are variations
that are added to this basic recipe for homemade cookies
as fast as you can open the oven door. You'll be amazed at
the variety of cookies made from one simple dough.*

½ cup (1 stick) butter, softened	125 ml
1 cup sugar	250 ml
1 egg	1
½ teaspoon vanilla	2 ml
½ teaspoon salt	2 ml
1 teaspoon baking powder	5 ml
2 cups flour	500 ml

1. In large bowl, cream butter and sugar. Add egg and vanilla and beat until light and fluffy.

2. In medium bowl, sift salt, baking powder and flour together. Gradually add to butter mixture, beating well after each addition.

3. Cover and refrigerate dough until ready to use. Warm to room temperature before using unless recipe specifies otherwise.

**USE THIS BASIC COOKIE DOUGH TO MAKE
ANY OF THE RECIPES ON PAGES 7-11.**

Chocolate-Topped Brownie Bites

Looking and tasting like little bits of brownie, these cookies are fast to make and disappear even faster.

1 recipe *Basic Cookie Dough* (page 6)	1
4 tablespoons cocoa powder	60 ml
½ cup milk	125 ml
½ cup chopped nuts	125 ml
1 cup shredded coconut	250 ml

1. Preheat oven to 350° (176° C) In medium bowl, combine **Basic Cookie Dough** (page 6) with cocoa powder and milk.

2. Beat on low speed to blend. Stir in nuts and coconut.

3. Drop by rounded teaspoonfuls onto lightly greased cookie sheet. Bake for 10 minutes.

4. Remove from oven and cool cookies on cookie sheet for 1 minute, then transfer to cooling rack. When cool, spoon about 1 teaspoon (5 ml) chocolate glaze over the top of each cookie.

5. Let chocolate set before serving or storing. Makes 4 to 4½ dozen.

Chocolate Glaze:

1 cup semi-sweet chocolate chips	250 ml
6 tablespoons butter	90 ml

1. Combine chocolate and butter in small saucepan and melt over very low heat, stirring constantly until mixture is smooth. Remove from heat and use immediately.

Spicy Pineapple Cookies

1 recipe *Basic Cookie Dough* (page 6)	1
1 teaspoon cinnamon	5 ml
½ teaspoon ground nutmeg	2 ml
¼ teaspoon ground cloves	1 ml
⅔ cup crushed pineapple, very well drained	160 ml

1. Preheat oven to 375° (190° C). In medium bowl, combine **Basic Cookie Dough** (page 6) with cinnamon, nutmeg, cloves and pineapple. Beat until dough thoroughly blends.

2. Drop by heaping teaspoonfuls onto ungreased cookie sheet. Bake for 13 to 15 minutes or until edges are light brown.

3. Remove from oven and cool cookies on cookie sheet for 1 minute, then transfer to cooling rack. (Makes 3½ to 4 dozen.)

Mocha-Chip Drops

*These light cookies have a delicate mocha flavor
and are studded with chocolate chips.*

1 teaspoon instant coffee	5 ml
2 tablespoons half-and-half or milk	30 ml
1 recipe *Basic Cookie Dough* (page 6)	1
½ cup shortening	125 ml
½ teaspoon almond extract	2 ml
1 cup mini-chocolate chips	250 ml

1. Preheat oven to 375° (190° C). In small bowl, stir coffee into half-and-half to dissolve. Set aside.

2. In medium bowl, combine **Basic Cookie Dough** (page 6) with shortening, almond extract and coffee mixture. Beat until dough blends well. Stir in chocolate chips.

3. Drop by heaping teaspoonfuls onto ungreased cookie sheet. Bake for 10 minutes. Remove from oven and cool cookies on cookie sheet for 1 minute, then transfer to cooling rack. (Makes 4 to 4½ dozen.)

Maple-Iced Walnut Drops

Real maple syrup is the key to making these tasty cookies. It gives the icing a strong maple flavor that complements the walnuts in the cookies. These take very little time to make, especially if you whip up the icing while the first batch is baking.

1 recipe *Basic Cookie Dough* (page 6)	1
2 cups coarsely chopped walnuts	500 ml

1. Preheat oven to 350° (176° C). In medium bowl, mix walnuts with *Basic Cookie Dough* (page 6).

2. Drop by heaping teaspoonfuls onto ungreased cookie sheet. Bake for 10 to 12 minutes or until light brown around edges.

3. Remove from oven, cool cookies on cookie sheet for 1 minute and transfer to cooling rack. When cool, frost with maple icing.

Maple Icing:

3 tablespoons butter, softened	45 ml
1½ cups powdered sugar	375 ml
¼ cup maple syrup	60 ml

1. Combine butter, powdered sugar and maple syrup in medium bowl. Beat until well blended and mixture is smooth.

2. Frost when cookies are cool.

White Chocolate Rounds

1 recipe *Basic Cookie Dough* (page 6)	1
¼ cup shortening	60 ml
¼ cup packed brown sugar	60 ml
1 tablespoon milk	15 ml
1 cup white chocolate chips	250 ml
1 cup chopped maraschino cherries, drained	250 ml

1. Preheat oven to 375° (190° C). In large bowl, combine **Basic Cookie Dough** (page 6) with shortening, brown sugar and milk, Beat until well blended. Stir in white chocolate chips and cherries. Drop by heaping teaspoonfuls onto ungreased cookie sheet.

2. Bake for 10 to 12 minutes, just until edges begin to brown. Remove from oven and cool cookies on cookie sheet for 1 minute. Transfer to cooling rack. (Makes 3 to 4 dozen.)

Hearty Carrot Cookies

1 recipe *Basic Cookie Dough* (page 6)	1
½ cup packed brown sugar	125 ml
1 cup shredded, peeled carrots	250 ml
1 teaspoon cinnamon	5 ml
½ teaspoon ground nutmeg	2 ml
2 cups quick-cooking oats	500 ml
1 cup raisins	250 ml
1 cup coarsely chopped walnuts or pecans	250 ml

1. Preheat oven to 375° (190° C). In large bowl, combine **Basic Cookie Dough** (page 6) with brown sugar, carrots, cinnamon and nutmeg. Beat until well blended. Beat in oats. Stir in raisins and nuts.

2. Drop by heaping teaspoonfuls onto lightly greased cookie sheet and bake for 10 minutes or until light brown around edges.

3. Remove from oven and cool cookies on cookie sheet for 1 minute, then transfer to cooling rack. (Makes 4½ to 5 dozen.)

Brandied-Fruitcake Cookies

*This hearty, holiday cookie that's big on fruitcake flavor.
These will appeal to those who like fruitcake flavor but aren't
crazy about spices. They have a moist texture and their light
color lets the colorful fruits and nuts show through.*

½ cup brandy	125 ml
1 cup fruitcake mix (candied fruit)	250 ml
1 recipe *Basic Cookie Dough* (page 6)	1
1 tablespoon buttermilk	15 ml
1 teaspoon orange extract	10 ml
1 cup chopped pecans	250 ml
1 cup raisins	250 ml

1. In small saucepan, heat brandy almost to boiling. Pour over fruitcake mix and let sit for 20 minutes. Drain and reserve brandy. Set fruit aside.

2. Preheat oven to 375° (190° C). In medium bowl, combine **Basic Cookie Dough** (page 6) with reserved brandy, buttermilk and orange extract. Beat until dough blends well. Stir in fruit, pecans and raisins.

3. Drop by heaping teaspoonfuls onto lightly greased cookie sheet. Bake for 10 to 12 minutes or until light brown around edges.

4. Remove from oven and cool cookies on cookie sheet for 1 minute, then transfer to cooling rack. (Makes 4 to 5 dozen.)

Apricot Cookies

1½ cups (3 sticks) butter, softened	375 ml
2 cups sugar	500 ml
1 (8 ounce) package cream cheese, softened	1 (228 g)
2 eggs, beaten	2
2 tablespoons lemon juice	30 ml
2 tablespoons lemon zest	30 ml
4½ cups flour	1 L + 125 ml
1½ teaspoons baking powder	7 ml
1 (16 ounce) jar apricot preserves	1 (454 g)
Powdered sugar	

1. In mixing bowl, combine butter, sugar and cream cheese and beat until smooth and fluffy. Blend in eggs, juice and lemon zest.

2. Stir in flour and baking powder and mix well. Chill dough in refrigerator several hours.

3. With tablespoon, shape dough in balls and place on ungreased baking sheet.

4. With back of spoon, flatten each ball slightly and make indention in center of each cookie, then fill with apricot preserves.

5. Bake at 350° (176° C) about 15 minutes. (Cookies do not need to brown.)

6. Cool and sprinkle with powdered sugar.

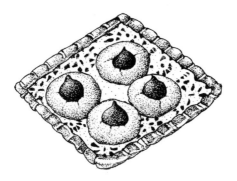

Mairzy D' Oats

½ cup (1 stick) butter	125 ml
2 (1 ounce) squares semi-sweet chocolate	2 (28 g)
18 large marshmallows	18
2 cups flour	500 ml
2 tablespoons water	30 ml
1 teaspoon vanilla	5 ml
1 cup oats	250 ml
1 cup very finely chopped pecans	250 ml
Candied cherries	

1. Preheat oven to 350° (176° C).

2. In large saucepan over very low heat, melt butter, chocolate and marshmallows and stir until mixture is smooth and ingredients blend well.

3. Add flour, water, vanilla and oats and mix well.

4. Shape dough in balls and roll each ball in finely chopped pecans.

5. Press cherry into each ball and place on ungreased baking sheets. Bake about 20 minutes.

6. Cool and store in airtight container.

Chocolate-Filled Thumbprints

1 cup (2 sticks) butter, softened	250 ml
½ cup sugar	125 ml
¼ teaspoon salt	1 ml
2 egg yolks	2
1 tablespoon vanilla	15 ml
2¼ cups flour	560 ml
Coarse white sugar	
1 cup chocolate chips	250 ml

1. Preheat oven to 350° (176° C).

2. In mixing bowl, combine butter, sugar, salt, egg yolks and vanilla and beat well. Fold in flour.

3. Scoop mixture in 2-teaspoon (10 ml) portions and gently roll to make 1-inch (2.5 cm) balls.

4. On parchment-lined baking sheets, place balls and use thumb to make indention in each cookie.

5. Roll edges of each cookie in coarse white sugar. Bake 10 minutes and remove from oven.

6. Press center of each cookie again with end of wooden spoon.

7. Return to oven and bake 10 to 12 minutes more. Melt chocolate chips and spoon melted chocolate in each indention.

(Continued on next page.)

(Continued)

Optional Peanut Butter Filling:

1 (3 ounce) package cream cheese, softened	1 (85 g)
¾ cup creamy peanut butter	180 ml
½ cup powdered sugar	125 ml
1 tablespoon milk	15 ml
1 teaspoon vanilla	5 ml

In mixing bowl, combine all ingredients and fill baked cookies.

Peanut Butter Snaps

1 (18 ounce) roll refrigerated peanut butter cookie dough	1 (520 g)
1 (9 ounce) bag miniature Reese's peanut butter cups	1 (240 g)

1. Preheat oven to 350° (176° C).

2. Cut roll of cookies in 9 slices. Cut each slice in quarters.

3. Roll dough in balls and press into miniature muffin pan.

4. Bake 10 to 12 minutes. (Cookies will form a tiny crust like a pie shell.)

5. Remove paper from peanut butter cups.

6. As soon as cookies come out of oven, insert peanut butter cup into center of each cookie.

7. Cool before removing from pan.

Cherry Treats

1 cup (2 sticks) butter, softened	250 ml
1 (3 ounce) package cream cheese, softened	1 (85 g)
1½ cups sugar	375 ml
1 egg, separated	1
1 teaspoon almond extract	5 ml
2½ cups flour	625 ml
1 cup finely ground slivered almonds	250 ml
32 red candied cherries, halved	32

1. In mixing bowl, beat butter, cream cheese and sugar until creamy.

2. Add egg yolk and almond extract and mix well. Gradually stir in flour.

3. Cover and chill several hours.

4. Shape dough in 1-inch (2.5 cm) balls. In small bowl, lightly beat egg white. Dip tops of dough in egg white and then in slivered almonds.

5. On lightly greased baking sheet, place dough balls 2 inches apart and press cherry half in center of each ball.

6. Bake at 350° (176° C) for 12 to 15 minutes. (Cookies do not need to brown.)

7. Store in airtight container and chill.

Cherry-Yuletide Cookies

½ cup (1 stick) butter, softened 125 ml
¾ cup powdered sugar 180 ml
1 egg, separated 1
½ teaspoon vanilla 2 ml
1½ cups flour 375 ml
¼ teaspoon salt 1 ml
2 tablespoons sugar 30 ml
Candied cherries

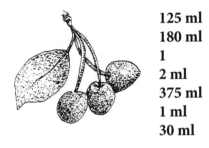

1. In mixing bowl, combine butter, powdered sugar, egg yolk and vanilla and beat well.

2. Stir in flour and salt and mix well. Cover and chill several hours or overnight.

3. When ready to bake, preheat oven to 350° (176° C).

4. Using 1 teaspoon (5 ml) dough for each cookie, form dough into balls and place on ungreased baking sheet. With end of wooden spoon, make indention in center of each cookie.

5. Bake 12 to 14 minutes or until cookies brown lightly.

6. While cookies bake, beat egg white until very stiff while gradually adding sugar.

7. Remove cookies from oven and place small dab of beaten egg white in center.

8. Return cookies to oven to slightly brown meringue (about 5 minutes).

9. While cookies are still warm, place candied cherry on top of meringue. Cool and store in airtight container.

Holly-Almond Cookies

1 cup (2 sticks) butter, softened	250 ml
1 (3 ounce) package cream cheese, softened	1 (85 g)
1½ cups powdered sugar	375 ml
2 cups flour	500 ml
1 cup almonds, finely chopped	250 ml
2 teaspoons almond flavoring	10 ml
1 teaspoon vanilla	5 ml
3½ (16 ounce) packages whole candied cherries	3½ (454 g)

1. Preheat oven to 325° (163° C).

2. In mixing bowl, blend butter, cream cheese and sugar. Add flour gradually and mix well.

3. Stir in almonds, almond flavoring and vanilla and mix well.

4. With spoon of dough, form ball with hands. Push candied cherry down in center of each ball. Flatten each cookie slightly, but do not cover cherry.

5. Bake 20 to 25 minutes or until edges just begin to brown.

Sugared-Pretzel Cookies

2 (18 ounce) tubes refrigerated sugar cookie dough	2 (520 g)
1 (6 ounce) package white chocolate chips	1 (170 g)
1 (8 ounce) package white chocolate-covered pretzels	1 (228 g)

1. Preheat oven to 350° (176° C).

2. Crumble cookie dough into large bowl and stir in white chocolate chips. (Dough will be very stiff.) Drop by tablespoonfuls on ungreased cookie sheet.

3. Bake for 16 to 18 minutes until very light brown. Immediately press pretzel into center of each cookie. Cool on wire rack.

Chocolate-Peanut Butter Pinwheels

1 cup (2 sticks) butter, softened	250 ml
1 cup sugar	250 ml
1¼ cups packed brown sugar	310 ml
1 cup crunchy peanut butter	250 ml
2 eggs	2
2⅔ cups flour	660 ml
1 teaspoon baking soda	5 ml
¼ teaspoon salt	1 ml
1 (12 ounce) package chocolate chips	1 (340 g)
¼ cup (½ stick) butter	60 ml

1. In mixing bowl, cream butter, sugars, peanut butter and eggs and beat well.

2. Add flour, baking soda and salt and stir until ingredients mix well. Divide dough in half and chill.

3. On lightly floured wax paper, roll out each half into rectangle about 15 x 18 inches (38 x 46 cm).

4. In saucepan, melt chocolate chips and butter and quickly spread on both rectangles of dough.

5. Roll up to form logs 15 inches (38 cm) long. Wrap tightly and chill at least 1 hour.

6. Slice each log into cookies about ⅓ inch (.5) thick. On ungreased baking sheet, bake cookies at 350° (176° C) for 10 to 12 minutes.

Apricot-Stuffed Cookies

1 cup (2 sticks) butter, softened	250 ml
1 (8 ounce) package cream cheese, softened	1 (228 g)
4 tablespoons light brown sugar	60 ml
2 cups flour	500 ml
½ teaspoon baking powder	2 ml
2 cups finely chopped pecans	500 ml
1½ cups apricot preserves	375 ml
3 tablespoons sugar	45 ml
¼ cup powdered sugar	60 ml

1. In mixing bowl, cream butter and cream cheese until smooth.

2. In separate bowl, combine light brown sugar, flour and baking powder. Add to creamed mixture and mix well. Refrigerate dough several hours.

3. In small bowl, combine pecans, apricot preserves and 3 teaspoons (15 ml) sugar. Divide dough in 3 equal parts and roll dough very thin on lightly floured board. Cut dough in 2-inch circles (5 cm) and place on baking sheet.

4. Place 1 teaspoon (5 ml) pecan-apricot mixture in center of each cookie. Top with another circle. With floured tines of fork, press edges together.

5. Bake at 350° (176° C) for 15 to 18 minutes.

6. When cookies cool, sprinkle with powdered sugar.

Classic Oatmeal Sandwich Cookies

¾ cup (1½ sticks) butter or shortening, softened	180 ml
1¼ cups packed brown sugar	310 ml
1 egg	1
⅓ cup milk	80 ml
2 teaspoons vanilla	10 ml
3 cups quick-cooking oats	750 ml
1 cup flour	250 ml
½ teaspoon baking soda	2 ml
½ teaspoon salt	2 ml

Frosting:

2 cups powdered sugar	500 ml
¼ cup (½ stick) butter or shortening	60 ml
½ teaspoon vanilla	2 ml
Milk	

1. Preheat oven to 350° (176° C). Beat ¾ cup (180 ml) butter, brown sugar, egg, milk and vanilla until creamy. In a separate bowl, mix oats, flour, baking soda and salt. Add to butter mixture in several batches and beat until ingredients mix well.

2. Drop tablespoons of dough on greased cookie sheet and bake for about 13 minutes or until light brown. (The more you bake, the crispier the cookies are.) Allow cookies to cool completely.

3. Combine powdered sugar, ¼ cup (60 ml) butter or shortening and vanilla and beat at medium speed until frosting mixes well and reaches spreading consistency. Spread frosting on bottom of 1 cookie and top with the bottom of another cookie. Repeat process for all cookies.

Cobblestones

½ cup (1 stick) butter	125 ml
1 ounce unsweetened chocolate	28 g
1 cup sugar	250 ml
1 cup flour	250 ml
1 teaspoon baking powder	5 ml
1 teaspoon vanilla	5 ml
2 eggs	2
¾ cup chopped pecans	180 ml

Filling:

1 (8 ounce) package cream cheese, softened, divided	1 (228 g)
½ cup sugar	125 ml
¼ cup (½ stick) butter, softened	60 ml
2 tablespoons flour	30 ml
1 egg	1
½ cup chopped pecans	125 ml
1 (6 ounce) package semi-sweet chocolate chips	1 (170 g)
2 cups miniature marshmallows	500 ml

Frosting:

¼ cup (½ stick) butter	60 ml
2 ounces unsweetened chocolate	57 g
¼ cup milk	60 ml
3 cups powdered sugar	750 ml

1. Preheat oven to 350° (176° C).

2. In saucepan, melt butter and chocolate. Remove from heat and add sugar, flour, baking powder, vanilla, eggs and pecans and mix.

3. In greased, floured 9 x 13-inch (23 x 33 cm) baking pan, spread dough to form crust. Set aside.

(Continued on next page.)

(Continued)

4. To make filling, combine 6 ounces (170 g) cream cheese, sugar, butter, flour and egg in mixing bowl. Beat until fluffy and stir in pecans.

5. Spread cream cheese over first layer. Sprinkle with chocolate chips. Bake 35 minutes. Remove from oven, sprinkle with marshmallows and bake 2 minutes longer.

6. To make frosting, melt remaining cream cheese, butter, chocolate and milk in saucepan. Stir in powdered sugar until smooth. Spread frosting over top and swirl. Cool and cut into bars.

Classic Turtle Cookies

1 (18 ounce) package chocolate chip cookie dough	**1 (520 g)**
2 cups pecan halves	**500 ml**
20 to 22 caramels	**20 to 22**
2 tablespoons milk	**30 ml**

1. Preheat oven to 375° (190° C). Slice cookie dough in about ¼ to ½ inch (1.5 cm) thick pieces. Form into balls and place on ungreased cookie sheet several inches apart.

2. Arrange 5 pecan halves at base of each ball, 1 for the head, 2 for arms and 2 for legs (or, if you prefer 4 for legs). Bake for about 10 to 14 minutes or until edges are light brown.

3. Put caramels and milk in microwave-safe bowl and microwave on HIGH for about 1 minute, rotating and stirring several times, until caramels are creamy. Drizzle over cookies when they are cool.

Classic Candy Bar Cookies

Dough:

¾ cup (1½ sticks) butter	180 ml
¾ cup powdered sugar	180 ml
2 tablespoons evaporated milk	30 ml
1 teaspoon vanilla	5 ml
2 cups flour	500 ml

Caramel Filling:

1 (8 ounce) package vanilla caramels, unwrapped	1 (228 g)
⅓ cup evaporated milk	80 ml
¼ cup (½ stick) butter, melted	60 ml
1 cup powdered sugar	250 ml
1 cup chopped pecans	250 ml

Chocolate Frosting:

1 (6 ounce) package chocolate chips	1 (170 g)
¼ cup evaporated milk	60 ml
⅛ cup (¼ stick) butter	30 ml
1 teaspoon vanilla	5 ml
½ cup powdered sugar	125 ml

1. Preheat oven to 325° (163° C).

2. In mixing bowl, cream butter and sugar. Add milk and vanilla and mix. Blend in flour gradually.

3. Roll out dough, cut in 1½ x 1½-inch (4 x 4 cm) squares and place on baking sheet. Bake 12 to 15 minutes.

4. To make filling, melt caramels with milk in small saucepan over low heat. Remove from heat, add remaining filling ingredients and mix. Spread layer of filling over cookies.

(Continued on next page.)

(Continued)

6. To make frosting, combine chocolate chips and milk in small saucepan and melt over low heat. Remove from heat and add butter, vanilla and sugar. Spread frosting over caramel filling. Store in airtight container.

A Date with a Cookie

Dough:

½ cup (1 stick) butter, softened	125 ml
½ cup packed light brown sugar	125 ml
½ cup sugar	125 ml
1 egg, beaten	1
½ teaspoon vanilla	2 ml
2 cups flour	500 ml
½ teaspoon baking soda	2 ml
½ teaspoon salt	2 ml

Filling:

½ pound pitted, chopped dates	228 g
⅓ cup sugar	80 ml
⅓ cup water	80 ml
1 cup chopped pecans	250 ml

1. In mixing bowl, combine butter, both sugars, egg and vanilla and beat well. Add flour, baking soda and salt and mix well. Chill dough several hours or overnight. To make filling, combine dates, sugar and water in saucepan and cook over medium heat 5 minutes. Add pecans and cool.

2. When dough is thoroughly chilled, roll out as thin as possible. Spread cooled filling on dough and roll like jelly-roll. Wrap in wax paper and freeze.

3. Slice dough thinly while frozen. Place slices on baking sheet and bake at 350° (176° C) for 5 to 6 minutes or until cookies brown lightly.

Classic Chocolate Cookies

½ cup butter, softened	125 ml
1 cup sugar	250 ml
1 egg	1
1 tablespoon cream	15 ml
½ teaspoon vanilla	2 ml
1¼ cups flour	310 ml
⅓ cup cocoa	80 ml
¼ teaspoon salt	1 ml
1 teaspoon baking powder	5 ml

1. Preheat oven to 375° (190° C). Cream butter and slowly add sugar. Beat until light and fluffy.

2. Combine egg, cream and vanilla, add to butter mixture and beat to mix.

3. In a separate bowl, combine flour, baking powder and salt. Add a little flour mixture to butter mixture and mix after each addition.

4. Drop by teaspoon onto greased cookie sheet. Bake for about 8 to 10 minutes. Makes about 5 dozen.

Classic Toll House Chocolate Chip Cookies

The #1 cookie in America

2¼ cups flour	560 ml
1 teaspoon baking soda	5 ml
1 teaspoon salt	5 ml
1 cup (2 sticks) butter, softened	250 ml
¾ cup sugar	180 ml
¾ cup firmly packed brown sugar	180 ml
1 teaspoon vanilla	5 ml
2 eggs	2
1 (12 ounce) package Nestle semi-sweet chocolate morsels	1 (340 g)
1 cup chopped nuts	250 ml

1. Preheat oven to 375° (190° C). Combine flour, baking soda and salt in medium bowl and set aside. In large bowl combine butter, sugar, brown sugar and vanilla and stir until creamy.

2. Add eggs and mix thoroughly. Add flour mixture a little at a time and stir to mix well. Add chocolate morsels and nuts and mix.

3. Drop by rounded teaspoonfuls onto ungreased baking sheets. Bake at 350° (176° C) for about 8 minutes.

*C*hocolate chip cookies were accidentally invented in 1930 by Massachusetts innkeeper Ruth Wakefield as she was preparing cookies for her guests. Out of baker's chocolate, Ruth substituted a semi-sweet chocolate bar, a gift from a Mr. Andrew Nestle of the Nestle Chocolate Company. Ruth thought the chocolate pieces would melt during cooking. They did not and the result was a cookie studded with chocolate bits. Since Ruth and her husband ran the Toll House Inn, you know the rest of the story. As the cookie recipe became popular, the two entrepreneurs struck a deal. In exchange for free chocolate for her recipe, Ruth agreed to allow Nestle to print her new "Chocolate Crunch Cookie" recipe on its packaging. And the Toll House chocolate chip cookie was born.

Chocolate Chip Champs

½ cup (1 stick) butter, softened	125 ml
¼ cup shortening	60 ml
½ cup sugar	125 ml
⅓ cup firmly packed brown sugar	80 ml
1 egg	1
1 teaspoon vanilla	5 ml
1½ cups flour	375 ml
½ teaspoon baking soda	2 ml
½ teaspoon salt	2 ml
1 (6 ounce) package semi-sweet chocolate chips	1 (170 g)
½ cup chopped pecans	125 ml

1. Preheat oven to 350° (176° C).

2. In large mixing bowl with electric mixer, combine butter, shortening, both sugars, egg and vanilla.

3. Add flour, baking soda and salt and continue to beat. Stir in chocolate chips and pecans.

4. On greased baking sheet, drop dough by teaspoonfuls and bake 8 to 10 minutes.

5. Store in airtight container.

The original "chocolate chips" were chopped Nestle candy bars. Nestle introduced chocolate morsels in 1939.

The Ultimate Chocolate Chip Cookies

¾ cup shortening	180 ml
1¼ cups firmly packed brown sugar	225 ml
2 tablespoons milk	30 ml
2 teaspoons vanilla	10 ml
1 egg	1
1¾ cups flour	430 ml
1 teaspoon salt	5 ml
¾ teaspoon baking soda	4 ml
1 cup semi-sweet chocolate chips	250 ml
1 cup chopped pecans	250 ml

1. Preheat oven to 375° (190° C).

2. In large bowl, cream shortening, sugar, milk and vanilla and blend until creamy. Add egg and mix.

3. Add flour, salt and baking soda to creamed mixture and stir well. Stir in chocolate chips and pecans.

4. On ungreased baking sheet, drop dough by rounded tablespoonfuls.

5. Bake 10 minutes for chewy cookies and 11 to 13 minutes for crispy cookies.

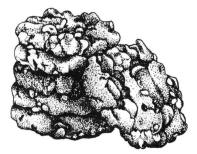

Krispie Chocolate Chip Cookies

1 cup (2 sticks) butter, softened	250 ml
½ cup packed brown sugar	125 ml
1 cup sugar	250 ml
2 eggs	2
1 teaspoon vanilla	5 ml
1 teaspoon baking soda	5 ml
½ teaspoon salt	2 ml
2¼ cups flour	560 ml
½ cup flaked coconut	125 ml
1 (12 ounce) package chocolate chips	1 (340 g)
½ cup chopped pecans	125 ml
1 cup crispy rice cereal	250 ml

1. Preheat oven to 350° (176° C).

2. In mixing bowl, cream butter, sugar, egg and vanilla and beat well. Add soda, salt and flour and mix well.

3. Stir in coconut, chocolate chips, pecans and crispy rice cereal and mix well.

4. On ungreased baking sheet, drop dough by teaspoonfuls and bake about 13 minutes or until cookies brown lightly.

5. Cool to room temperature before storing.

Peanutty Chippy-Chocolate Cookies

1 cup shortening	250 ml
1 cup sugar	250 ml
1 cup packed brown sugar	250 ml
2 eggs	2
2 teaspoons vanilla	10 ml
2 cups flour	500 ml
½ teaspoon baking powder	2 ml
½ teaspoon baking soda	2 ml
1 (6 ounce) package milk chocolate chips	1(170 g)
1 (12 ounce) package peanut butter chips	1(340 g)
3 cups crispy rice cereal	750 ml

1. Preheat oven to 350° (176° C).

2. In mixing bowl, combine shortening, both sugars, eggs and vanilla and beat well.

3. Add flour, baking powder and baking soda and mix well. Stir in chocolate chips, peanut butter chips and cereal and mix well.

4. On ungreased baking sheet, drop dough by teaspoonfuls and bake 10 to 12 minutes. Cool.

Crunchy Chocolate Olé Cookies

¼ cup (½ stick) butter, softened	60 ml
¼ cup shortening	60 ml
¼ cup crunchy peanut butter	60 ml
½ cup sugar	125 ml
¾ cup packed light brown sugar	180 ml
1 egg	1
1 teaspoon vanilla	5 ml
1¾ cups flour	430 ml
½ teaspoon baking soda	2 ml
½ teaspoon salt	2 ml
1 cup Spanish peanuts, chopped	250 ml
1 (6 ounce) package semi-sweet chocolate chips	1(170 g)

1. Preheat oven to 350° (176° C).

2. In mixing bowl, cream butter, shortening, peanut butter, both sugars, egg and vanilla and beat well.

3. Gradually add dry ingredients and mix well. Stir in peanuts and chocolate chips.

4. On ungreased baking sheets, drop dough by teaspoonfuls and bake 8 to 10 minutes or until edges of cookies turn light brown.

5. Cool cookies and store in airtight container.

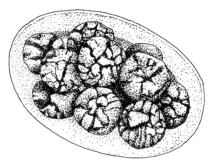

Classic Chocolate Chip-Peanut Butter Cookies

1 cup (2 sticks) butter, softened	250 ml
1 cup packed brown sugar	250 ml
1½ cups sugar	375 ml
2 eggs, beaten	2
1 cup chunky peanut butter	250 ml
3 cups flour	750 ml
1 teaspoon baking soda	5 ml
1 teaspoon baking powder	5 ml
¼ teaspoon salt	1 ml
1 cup chocolate chips	250 ml
1 cup peanut butter chips	250 ml

1. Preheat oven to 350° (176° C).

2. In mixing bowl, combine butter and both sugars and beat until creamy.

3. Add eggs one at a time and beat well after each addition. Fold in peanut butter and mix well.

4. In separate bowl, combine flour, baking soda, baking powder and salt. Stir dry ingredients into butter-peanut butter mixture and mix well.

5. Fold in chocolate chips and peanut butter chips and mix well.

6. On lightly greased baking sheet, drop batter by tablespoonfuls and bake 12 to 14 minutes or until cookies turn golden brown.

7. Cool before storing.

World's Greatest Cookies

5 cups oats, divided	1 L + 250 ml
2 cups (4 sticks) butter	500 ml
2 cups sugar	500 ml
2 cups packed brown sugar	500 ml
4 eggs	4
2 teaspoons vanilla	10 ml
4 cups flour	1 L
1 teaspoon salt	5 ml
2 teaspoons baking powder	10 ml
2 teaspoons baking soda	10 ml
2 (12 ounce) packages semi-sweet chocolate chips or white chocolate chips	2 (340 g)
1 (8 ounce) chocolate candy bar, grated	1 (228 g)
3 cups chopped pecans	750 ml

1. Preheat oven at 350° (176° C).

2. With blender or food processor, process 2½ cups (625 ml) oats to fine powder. Pour in bowl and repeat with remaining oats. Set aside.

3. In large mixing bowl, cream butter and both sugars. Stir in eggs and vanilla and beat well.

4. In separate bowl, combine flour, blended oats, baking powder and baking soda. Add to creamed mixture and mix well.

5. Stir in chocolate chips, grated candy bar and pecans.

6. Roll dough in balls and place 2 inches (5 cm) apart on baking sheet.

7. Bake 6 to 8 minutes.

Choc-O-Cherry Cookies

½ cup (1 stick) butter, softened	125 ml
1 cup sugar	250 ml
1 egg	1
½ teaspoon vanilla	2 ml
1½ cups flour	375 ml
½ cup cocoa	125 ml
¼ teaspoon salt	1 ml
¼ teaspoon baking powder	1 ml
¼ teaspoon baking soda	1 ml
1 (10 ounce) jar maraschino cherries, well drained	1(284 g)
1 (6 ounce) package chocolate chips	1(170 g)

1. Preheat oven to 350° (176° C).

2. In mixing bowl, cream butter, sugar, egg and vanilla until light and fluffy.

3. In separate bowl, add flour, cocoa, salt, baking powder and baking soda and gradually add to sugar mixture.

4. Cut cherries in quarters and add to batter. Add chocolate chips and mix.

5. On ungreased cookie sheet, drop dough by teaspoonfuls and bake 15 minutes.

Chocolate Kisses

2 egg whites, room temperature	**2**
⅔ cup sugar	**160 ml**
1 teaspoon vanilla	**5 ml**
Dash salt	
1¼ cups chopped pecans	**225 ml**
1 (6 ounce) package chocolate chips	**1(170 g)**

1. Preheat oven to 375° (190° C).

2. In mixing bowl, beat egg whites until very stiff. Blend in sugar, vanilla and salt.

3. Fold in pecans and chocolate chips.

4. Cover baking sheet with foil (shiny side up) and drop dough by rounded teaspoonfuls on foil.

5. TURN OVEN OFF and leave overnight.

6. If cookies are a little sticky the next day, leave out in air to dry.

In 1939 the Nestle Company made an agreement with the creator of the chocolate chip cookie to include the recipe on every package of chocolate morsels for 40 years. The recipe continues to be on the package to this day.

Chocolate-Mint Drops

¾ cup (1½ sticks) butter, softened	180 ml
1 cup powdered sugar	250 ml
2 tablespoons cocoa	30 ml
1½ cups flour	375 ml
¼ teaspoon peppermint extract	1 ml
1 (6 ounce) package semi-sweet chocolate chips	1 (170 g)

Icing:

¼ cup (½ stick) butter, softened	60 ml
1½ cups powdered sugar	375 ml
About 2 tablespoons milk	30 ml
¼ teaspoon peppermint extract	1 ml
2 to 3 drops green food coloring	2 to 3

1. In mixing bowl, beat butter and sugar until creamy. Stir in cocoa, flour and peppermint extract.

2. Stir in chocolate chips and drop by tablespoonfuls 2 inches (5 cm) apart on ungreased baking sheet.

3. Bake at 350° (176° C) for 8 to 9 minutes. Cool on wire rack.

4. For icing, combine, butter and powdered sugar and stir in just enough milk to make mixture spreadable. Add peppermint extract and food coloring and ice cookies.

Classic Hello Dollies

1½ cups graham cracker crumbs	375 ml
1 (6 ounce) package chocolate chips	1 (170 g)
1 cup flaked coconut	250 ml
1¼ cups chopped pecans	310 ml
1 (14 ounce) can sweetened condensed milk	1 (420 g)

1. Preheat oven to 350° (176° C). In 9 x 9-inch (23 x 23 cm) pan, sprinkle cracker crumbs to form crust. Layer chocolate chips, coconut and pecans over crust.

2. Pour condensed milk over layered ingredients.   Bake 25 to 30 minutes. Cool and cut in squares.

Three-Minute Cookies

1 (12 ounce) package milk chocolate chips	1 (340 g)
1 (14 ounce) can sweetened condensed milk	1 (420 g)
½ cup (1 stick) butter	125 ml
1 cup chopped pecans	250 ml
1 teaspoon vanilla	5 ml
1 cup flour	250 ml

1. Preheat oven to 350° (176° C). In double boiler over low heat, melt chocolate chips, sweetened condensed milk and butter. Remove from heat and add pecans, vanilla and flour.

2. On greased baking sheet, drop dough by teaspoonfuls and bake 11 to 13 minutes.

3. Cool on baking sheet about 3 minutes. Remove to cake rack to cool completely.

Krispie Snacks

1 cup (2 sticks) butter, softened	250 ml
¾ cup packed brown sugar	180 ml
1 cup sugar	250 ml
2 eggs	2 ml
2 teaspoons vanilla	10 ml
1 teaspoon baking soda	5 ml
½ teaspoon baking powder	2 ml
½ teaspoon salt	2 ml
2 cups flour	500 ml
1 cup flaked coconut	250 ml
1 (12 ounce) package chocolate chips	1(340 g)
2 cups crispy rice cereal	500 ml
½ cup chopped pecans	125 ml

1. Preheat oven to 350° (176° C).

2. In mixing bowl, cream butter, both sugars, eggs and vanilla and beat well.

3. Add baking soda, baking powder, salt and flour and mix well. Stir in remaining ingredients and mix well.

4. On greased baking sheet, drop dough by teaspoonfuls and bake about 10 minutes.

5. Cool and store in airtight container.

Monster Cookies

½ cup (1 stick) butter, softened	125 ml
1 cup sugar	250 ml
1½ cups packed brown sugar	375 ml
3 eggs	3
1¾ cups crunchy peanut butter	430 ml
½ teaspoon vanilla	2 ml
4½ cups oats	1 L 125 ml
2 teaspoons baking soda	10 ml
¼ teaspoon salt	1 ml
1 cup plain M&M candies	250 ml
1 (6 ounce) package semi-sweet chocolate chips	1(170 g)

1. Preheat oven to 350° (176° C).

2. In mixing bowl, cream butter, both sugars, eggs, peanut butter and vanilla and beat well.

3. Add oats, baking soda and salt and mix well.   Stir in M&M's and chocolate chips.

4. Pack dough in ¼ cup (60 ml) measuring cup and drop dough 4 inches (10 cm) apart on lightly greased baking sheets.

5. Dip spoon in water and lightly press each cookie to form circle.

6. Bake 14 to 16 minutes or until cookies brown slightly. Cool.

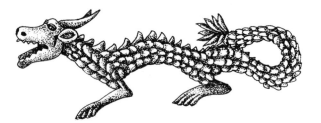

Classic Coconut-Chocolate Chip Cookies

Everybody's Favorite Cookies

1 cup (2 sticks) butter, softened	250 ml
1 cup sugar	250 ml
1½ cups packed light brown sugar	375 ml
2 eggs, beaten	2
2 teaspoons vanilla	10 ml
2½ cups flour	625 ml
1 teaspoon baking soda	5 ml
1 teaspoon baking powder	5 ml
¾ teaspoon salt	4 ml
1 cup flaked coconut	250 ml
1 (12 ounce) package milk chocolate chips	1 (340 g)
1 cup chopped pecans	250 ml

1. In mixing bowl, cream butter and both sugars. Add eggs and vanilla and beat well.

2. Fold in flour, baking soda, baking powder and salt and mix well. Stir in coconut, chocolate chips and pecans. Dough will be stiff.

3. Shape 3 tablespoons (45 ml) dough into balls and place 3 inches apart on ungreased cookie sheet.

4. Bake at 350° (176° C) for about 14 to 16 minutes or until light brown. Remove to wire rack to cool.

Nestle Chocolate Company originally sold a mini-chocolate chopper with its chocolate bars so customers could make Ruth Wakefield's cookie recipe.

Chocolate-Coconut Drops

1 cup sweetened condensed milk	250 ml
4 cups flaked coconut	1 L
⅔ cup mini semi-sweet chocolate bits	160 ml
1 teaspoon vanilla	5 ml
½ teaspoon almond extract	2 ml

1. Preheat oven to 325° (163° C).

2. In mixing bowl, combine milk and coconut to form gooey mixture.

3. Add chocolate bits, vanilla and almond extract and stir until ingredients mix well.

4. On sprayed baking sheet, drop dough by teaspoonfuls and bake 12 minutes.

5. Store in airtight container.

Chips Ahoy! Cookies were first put on the market in 1963.

Sierra Nuggets

1 cup (2 sticks) butter	250 ml
1 cup packed brown sugar	250 ml
1½ cups sugar	375 ml
1 tablespoon milk	15 ml
2 teaspoons vanilla	10 ml
2 eggs	2
1 cup crushed corn flakes	250 ml
3 cups oats	750 ml
1½ cups flour	375 ml
1¼ teaspoons baking soda	6 ml
1 teaspoon salt	5 ml
2 teaspoons cinnamon	10 ml
¼ teaspoon nutmeg	1 ml
⅛ teaspoon cloves	.5 ml
½ cup flaked coconut	125 ml
2 cups chocolate chips	500 ml
1 cup chopped walnuts or pecans	250 ml

1. Preheat oven to 350° (176° C).

2. In large mixing bowl, cream butter and both sugars and beat in milk, vanilla and eggs. Stir in corn flakes and oatmeal.

3. In separate bowl, sift flour, baking soda, salt and seasonings and gradually add to cookie mixture.

4. Stir in coconut, chocolate chips and nuts.

5. On baking sheet, drop dough by teaspoonfuls and bake 10 to 15 minutes.

Best-Ever Cookies

1½ cups sugar	375 ml
1 cup packed brown sugar	250 ml
1 (3.4 ounce) box instant vanilla pudding mix	1 (90 g)
¾ cup (1½ sticks) butter, softened	180 ml
1 cup oil	250 ml
2 eggs, beaten	2
3½ cups flour	875 ml
1 cup oats	250 ml
1 teaspoon salt	5 ml
1 teaspoon baking powder	5 ml
1 teaspoon baking soda	5 ml
1 cup crispy rice cereal	250 ml
1 cup chocolate chips	250 ml

1. Preheat oven to 350° (176° C).

2. In large bowl, combine both sugars, pudding mix, butter, oil and eggs and mix well.

3. Stir in remaining ingredients and mix well.

4. On greased baking sheet, drop dough by teaspoonfuls and bake until cookies brown slightly. Cool.

Cowboy Cookies

2 cups flour	500 ml
1 teaspoon baking soda	5 ml
½ teaspoon baking powder	2 ml
½ teaspoon salt	2 ml
1 cup (2 sticks) butter, softened	250 ml
1 cup sugar	250 ml
1 cup packed brown sugar	250 ml
2 eggs	2
1 teaspoon vanilla	5 ml
2 cups quick-cooking oats	500 ml
1 (6 ounce) package chocolate chips	1(170 g)
1 cup chopped pecans	250 ml

1. Preheat oven to 350° (176° C).

2. In mixing bowl, combine flour, soda, baking powder and salt and set aside.

3. In separate bowl, cream butter, both sugars, eggs and vanilla until fluffy. Add flour mixture and mix well.

4. Add oats, chocolate chips and pecans and mix well.

5. On greased baking sheet, drop dough by teaspoonfuls and bake about 15 minutes.

Chocolate-Mint Cookies

1 cup packed brown sugar	250 ml
¾ cup sugar	180 ml
1 cup (2 sticks) butter, softened	250 ml
1 teaspoon vanilla	5 ml
1 egg	1
1¾ cups flour	430 ml
¼ cup cocoa	60 ml
1 teaspoon baking soda	5 ml
½ teaspoon salt	2 ml
1 (6 ounce) package chocolate-mint chips	1(170 g)
¾ cup chopped pecans	180 ml

1. Preheat oven to 350° (176° C).

2. In mixing bowl, cream both sugars, butter, vanilla and egg and beat well.

3. In separate bowl, combine flour, cocoa, baking soda and salt. Gradually add to sugar mixture and mix well.

4. Stir in chocolate-mint chips and pecans.

5. On ungreased baking sheet, drop dough by teaspoonfuls and bake 7 to 10 minutes.

6. Cool and store in airtight container.

Pixies

1 cup (2 sticks) butter, softened	250 ml
1 cup crunchy peanut butter	250 ml
1 cup sugar	250 ml
1 cup packed brown sugar	250 ml
2 eggs	2
2¼ cups flour	560 ml
1 teaspoon baking soda	5 ml
1 (6 ounce) package milk chocolate chips	1(170 g)
¾ cup chopped pecans	180 ml

1. Preheat oven to 350° (176° C). In mixing bowl, cream butter, peanut butter, both sugars and eggs and beat well. Add flour and baking soda and mix well. Stir in chocolate chips and pecans.

2. On greased baking sheet, drop dough by teaspoonfuls. Dip spoon in water and flatten each cookie slightly. Bake 12 to 15 minutes and cool. Store in airtight container.

Chocolate-Crunch Cookies

1 (18 ounce) package German chocolate cake mix with pudding	1 (520 g)
1 egg, slightly beaten	1
½ cup (1 stick) butter, melted	125 ml
1 cup crispy rice cereal	250 ml

1. Preheat oven to 350° (176° C). In mixing bowl, combine cake mix, egg and butter. Add cereal and stir until it mixes well.

2. Shape dough in 1-inch (2.5 cm) balls and place on lightly greased baking sheet. Dip fork in flour and flatten cookies in criss-cross pattern. Bake 10 to 12 minutes and cool.

White Chocolate Almond Cookies

½ cup (1 stick) butter, softened	125 ml
½ cup packed brown sugar	125 ml
⅓ cup sugar	80 ml
1 egg	1
½ teaspoon almond extract	2 ml
1 cup plus 2 tablespoons flour	280 ml
½ teaspoon baking soda	2 ml
¼ teaspoon salt	1 ml
½ cup chopped blanched almonds	125 ml
8 ounces white chocolate chips or almond bark chips	1(228 g)

1. Preheat oven to 350° (176° C).

2. In large mixing bowl, cream butter and both sugars. Beat in egg and almond extract.

3. Add flour, baking soda and salt and mix well. Stir in almonds and chocolate.

4. On greased baking sheet, drop dough by rounded teaspoonfuls and bake 10 to 12 minutes or until cookies brown lightly.

5. Cool and store in covered container.

Macadamia Crunchies

1 cup (2 sticks) butter, softened	250 ml
½ cup packed brown sugar	125 ml
½ cup sugar	125 ml
2 eggs, beaten	2
1 teaspoon vanilla	5 ml
2¼ cups flour	560 ml
1 (3.4 ounce) package instant vanilla pudding mix	1(95 g)
1 teaspoon baking soda	5 ml
¼ teaspoon salt	1 ml
1 (12 ounce) package white chocolate chips	1(340 g)
1 cup chopped macadamia nuts	250 ml
½ cup finely crushed peanut brittle	125 ml

1. Preheat oven to 375° (190° C).

2. In mixing bowl, cream butter and both sugars until creamy.

3. Add eggs one at a time and beat well after each addition. Stir in vanilla.

4. In separate bowl, combine flour, instant pudding mix, baking soda and salt. Gradually add to creamed mixture and stir well.

5. Add chips, nuts and peanut brittle and stir to mix.

6. On greased baking sheet, drop dough by rounded tablespoonfuls and bake 10 to 12 minutes or until cookies brown lightly.

7. Cool before storing.

Macadamia Nut Cookies

½ cup shortening	125 ml
½ cup (1 stick) butter, softened	125 ml
2½ cups flour, divided	625 ml
1 cup packed brown sugar	250 ml
½ cup sugar	125 ml
2 eggs	2
1 teaspoon vanilla	5 ml
½ teaspoon butter flavoring	2 ml
1 teaspoon baking soda	5 ml
2 cups white chocolate chips	500 ml
1 (3½ ounce) jar macadamia nuts, chopped	1(95 g)

1. Preheat oven to 350° (176° C).

2. In mixing bowl, beat shortening and butter. Add half flour and mix well.

3. Add brown sugar, sugar, eggs, vanilla, butter flavoring and baking soda and beat until ingredients mix well.

4. Add remaining flour. Mix well and stir in chocolate pieces and nuts.

5. On ungreased baking sheet, drop dough by teaspoonfuls and bake about 8 minutes.

These are better than those good cookies you buy at the mall.

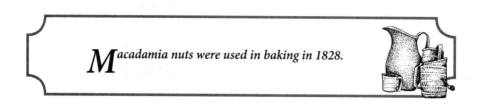

*M*acadamia nuts were used in baking in 1828.

Classic Peanut Butter Cookies

½ cup (1 stick) butter, softened	125 ml
¼ cup shortening	60 ml
1¼ cups chunky peanut butter	310 ml
½ cup sugar	125 ml
1 cup packed brown sugar	250 ml
1 egg	1
1½ cups flour	375 ml
½ teaspoon baking powder	2 ml
½ teaspoon baking soda	2 ml
½ teaspoon salt	2 ml
Sugar	

1. Preheat oven to 350° (176° C).

2. In large mixing bowl, cream butter, shortening, peanut butter, both sugars and egg and beat until fluffy. Add remaining ingredients and mix.

3. Use large cookie scoop to place cookies on baking sheet. Make cookies thicker and larger than most cookies.

4. Dip fork in sugar and flatten slightly with criss-cross pattern.

5. Bake for about 12 minutes.

*H*ow do you identify an "authentic" peanut butter cookie? By the criss-cross design on the top, of course! This interesting practice dates back to a 1931 edition of Pillsbury's "Balanced Recipes", which included "Peanut Butter Balls" flattened with a fork before baking. Even the most modern cooks wouldn't think of skipping this time-honored tradition. Peanut butter cookie dough is delightfully smooth and rolls easily. For generations, children have waited eagerly to "make the criss-cross" on dough balls bound for the oven.

Mother's Peanut Butter Cookies

2 cups (4 sticks) butter, softened	500 ml
1 cup creamy peanut butter	250 ml
¾ cup sugar	180 ml
1½ cups packed brown sugar	375 ml
2 eggs, beaten	2
1 teaspoon vanilla	5 ml
2½ cups flour	625 ml
2 teaspoons baking soda	10 ml
⅛ teaspoon salt	.5 ml
Sugar	

1. In mixing bowl, beat butter, peanut butter and both sugars until creamy. Add eggs and vanilla and beat well.

2. Stir in flour, baking soda and salt. Cover and chill several hours.

3. Shape dough in 1-inch (2.5 cm) balls and place on ungreased baking sheet. Dip fork in additional sugar and flatten cookies in criss-cross design.

4. Bake at 350° (176° C) for 7 to 9 minutes. Cool before storing.

Easy Peanut Butter Cookies

1 (18 ounce) package refrigerated sugar cookie dough	1(520 g)
½ cup creamy peanut butter	125 ml
½ cup miniature chocolate chips	125 ml
½ cup peanut butter chips	125 ml
½ cup chopped peanuts	125 ml

1. Preheat oven to 350° (176° C). In large mixing bowl, beat cookie dough and peanut butter until blended and smooth. Stir in remaining ingredients. On ungreased baking sheet, drop heaping tablespoonfuls of dough.

2. Dip fork in sugar and press down on each cookie in criss-cross design to flatten. Wet fork when necessary. Bake for 15 minutes and cool on rack.

Peanut Butter-Date Cookies

1 egg, beaten	1
⅔ cup sugar	160 ml
⅓ cup packed brown sugar	80 ml
1 cup chunky peanut butter	250 ml
½ cup chopped dates	125 ml

1. Preheat oven to 350° (176° C). In mixing bowl, blend egg, both sugars and peanut butter and mix thoroughly. Stir in dates.

2. Roll dough in 1-inch (2.5 cm) balls and place on ungreased baking sheet. With fork, flatten each ball to about ½-inch (1.5 cm) thick. Bake about 12 minutes and cool before storing.

Old-Fashioned Peanut Butter Cookies

1 cup shortening	250 ml
1 cup crunchy or creamy peanut butter	250 ml
1 cup packed brown sugar	250 ml
1 cup sugar	250 ml
1 teaspoon vanilla	5 ml
2 eggs, well beaten	2
2½ cups flour	625 ml
1 teaspoon baking soda	5 ml
1 teaspoon baking powder	5 ml
½ teaspoon salt	2 ml

1. Preheat oven to 350° (176° C). Cream shortening and peanut butter. Add brown sugar, sugar and vanilla and mix well. Stir in beaten eggs.

2. Combine flour, baking soda, baking powder and salt. Pour into peanut butter mixture in small batches and mix well after each addition.

3. Form into 1 to 2-inch (2.5 to 5 cm) balls and arrange on baking sheet about 2 inches (5 cm) apart. Dip fork into water and flatten slightly with tines of fork. Criss-cross pattern with fork to flatten a little more.

4. Bake for about 10 to 12 minutes.

Classic Peanut Butter Blossoms

½ cup shortening	125 ml
½ cup peanut butter	125 ml
½ cup packed brown sugar	125 ml
1 cup sugar, divided	250 ml
1 egg, beaten	1
1 teaspoon vanilla	5 ml
1¾ cups flour	430 ml
1 teaspoon baking soda	5 ml
½ teaspoon salt	2 ml
Chocolate stars or kisses	

1. Preheat oven to 350° (176° C). Mix shortening and peanut butter until creamy. Slowly mix in brown sugar, ½ cup (125 ml) sugar, egg and vanilla.

2. Mix flour, baking soda and salt and slowly add to peanut butter mixture, beating after each addition.

3. Shape into balls, roll in remaining sugar and place on cookie sheet. Bake for 8 minutes and remove from oven.

4. Put chocolate stars or kisses on each cookie and push down so cookie cracks. Return to oven and bake for 2 to 5 minutes longer.

Cinnamon-Peanut Cookies

½ cup (1 stick) butter, softened	125 ml
½ cup sugar	125 ml
½ cup packed brown sugar	125 ml
½ cup creamy peanut butter	125 ml
1 egg	1
1 teaspoon vanilla	5 ml
1 cup flour	250 ml
½ teaspoon salt	2 ml
1 teaspoon cinnamon	5 ml
½ cup chopped peanuts	125 ml

1. Preheat oven to 350° (176° C).

2. In mixing bowl, combine butter, both sugars, peanut butter, egg and vanilla and beat well.

3. Add flour, salt and cinnamon and mix well. Stir in peanuts.

4. On ungreased baking sheet, drop dough by teaspoonfuls and bake 10 to 12 minutes.

African-American scientist and educator George Washington Carver (1864-1943) revolutionized agriculture in the Southern states when he promoted the cultivation of peanuts as a substitute for cotton crops damaged by boll weevil infestations.

Apple-Chip Cookies

1 cup shortening	250 ml
1½ cups packed brown sugar	375 ml
⅓ cup light corn syrup	80 ml
2 eggs	2
3 cups flour	750 ml
½ teaspoon salt	2 ml
1 teaspoon baking soda	5 ml
1 teaspoon cinnamon	5 ml
¼ teaspoon ground cloves	1 ml
¼ teaspoon ground nutmeg	1 ml
¾ cup chopped walnuts	180 ml
1 cup peeled, grated cooking apples	250 ml
1 (6 ounce) package butterscotch morsels	1 (170 g)

1. Preheat oven to 350° (176° C).

2. In mixing bowl, cream shortening, brown sugar, corn syrup and eggs and beat well.

3. Add flour, salt, baking soda, cinnamon, cloves and nutmeg and mix well.

4. Stir in walnuts, apples and butterscotch morsels and mix well.

5. On greased baking sheet, drop dough by teaspoonfuls and bake 12 minutes or until cookies brown slightly.

Glazed-Apple Cookies

½ cup (1 stick) butter, softened	125 ml
1½ cups packed brown sugar	375 ml
1 egg	1
2 cups flour	500 ml
1 teaspoon salt	5 ml
1 teaspoon cinnamon	5 ml
½ teaspoon ground cloves	2 ml
¼ teaspoon nutmeg	1 ml
¼ cup apple juice	60 ml
1 cup chopped pecans	250 ml
1 cup raisins	250 ml
1 cup grated raw apple, unpared	250 ml

Glaze:

1 tablespoon butter, softened	15 ml
1½ cups powdered sugar	375 ml
2½ tablespoons apple juice	37 ml
¼ teaspoon vanilla	1 ml

1. Preheat oven to 350° (176° C).

2. In mixing bowl, cream butter and sugar. Add egg and beat well.

3. In separate bowl, combine flour, baking soda, salt, cinnamon, cloves and nutmeg. Add flour mixture and apple juice alternately to butter mixture. Stir in pecans and raisins and fold in apple.

4. On greased baking sheet, drop dough by teaspoonfuls and bake 10 to 12 minutes. Cool cookies on wire rack.

5. To make glaze, cream butter and sugar. Add apple juice and vanilla and mix well.

6. Spread glaze on cookies.

Applesauce Yummies

4 cups flour	1 L
2 teaspoons baking soda	10 ml
1 teaspoon salt	5 ml
1 teaspoon cinnamon	5 ml
1 teaspoon nutmeg	5 ml
½ teaspoon allspice	2 ml
1 cup (2 sticks) butter, softened	250 ml
1½ cups sugar	375 ml
1½ cups packed brown sugar	375 ml
3 eggs, beaten	3
2 cups applesauce	500 ml
1 cup golden raisins	250 ml
1½ cups chopped walnuts	375 ml

1. Preheat oven to 400° (204° C).

2. In mixing bowl, combine flour, baking soda, salt, cinnamon, nutmeg and allspice.

3. In separate bowl, combine butter and both sugars and beat with electric mixer until fluffy. Stir in eggs and applesauce.

4. Add dry ingredients and mix well. Stir in raisins and walnuts.

5. On greased baking sheet, drop dough by teaspoonfuls and bake 8 to 10 minutes or just until cookies brown lightly.

Banana Cookies

1½ cups flour	375 ml
1¼ cups sugar	310 ml
½ teaspoon baking soda	2 ml
½ teaspoon salt	2 ml
¼ teaspoon nutmeg	1 ml
¾ teaspoon cinnamon	4 ml
¾ cup shortening	180 ml
1 egg, beaten	1
1 cup mashed bananas	250 ml
1½ cups oats	375 ml
¾ cup chopped pecans	180 ml

1. Preheat oven to 375° (190° C).

2. In large bowl, combine flour, sugar, baking soda, salt, nutmeg and cinnamon.

3. Cut in shortening and add remaining ingredients. Beat well.

4. On ungreased baking sheet, drop dough by teaspoonfuls and bake about 15 minutes. Cool before storing.

Corn Flakes and Coconut Cookies

1 cup sugar	250 ml
1½ cups packed brown sugar	375 ml
1¼ cups (2½ sticks) butter, softened	310 ml
2 eggs, beaten	2
2 teaspoons vanilla	10 ml
2 cups flour	500 ml
2 teaspoons baking soda	10 ml
⅛ teaspoon salt	.5 ml
2 cups oats	500 ml
1 cup flaked coconut	250 ml
2½ cups corn flakes	625 ml

1. Preheat oven to 350° (176° C).

2. In mixing bowl, combine both sugars and butter and beat until creamy. Add eggs and vanilla and beat well.

3. Stir in flour, baking soda and salt. Stir by hand to fold in oats, coconut and corn flakes.

4. Shape dough in 1-inch (2.5 cm) balls and place on greased baking sheet. Bake 8 to 10 minutes.

5. Cool before storing.

Rich Date Cookies

1½ cups sugar, divided	375 ml
2 cups sliced pitted dates	500 ml
½ cup water	125 ml
4 cups flour	1 L
1 teaspoon baking soda	5 ml
1 teaspoon salt	5 ml
1 cup (2 sticks) butter, softened	250 ml
1 cup packed brown sugar	250 ml
3 eggs	3
1 teaspoon vanilla	5 ml
1½ cups chopped pecans	375 ml

1. Preheat oven to 350° (176° C).

2. In saucepan over medium heat, cook and stir ½ cup (125 ml) sugar, dates and ½ cup (125 ml) water until mixture thickens. Set aside to cool.

3. In large bowl, combine flour, baking soda and salt and set aside.

4. In separate bowl, cream butter, 1 cup (250 ml) sugar and brown sugar and mix well. Blend in eggs and vanilla.

5. Add dry ingredients and mix well. Stir in pecans and cooked dates.

6. On greased baking sheet, drop dough by teaspoonfuls and bake 12 to 14 minutes.

7. Cool and store in airtight container.

Classic Old-Fashioned Date-Log Cookies

1 cup dates	250 ml
¼ cup water	60 ml
¼ cup sugar	60 ml
1 (3 ounce) package cream cheese, softened	1 (85 g)
½ cup butter	125 ml
1 cup flour	250 ml
Dash salt	
Powdered sugar	

1. Preheat oven to 275°(135° C). Cook dates, water and sugar in saucepan over medium heat until a smooth paste forms. Blend cream cheese and butter until smooth. Add flour and salt and mix well. On lightly floured wax paper, roll out dough and cut in 3-inch (7.6 cm) squares.

2. Place 1 teaspoon (5 ml) date mixture on each square and roll up as logs. Seal ends with fork. Bake for 20 minutes. Roll in powdered sugar and serve.

Fruited-Date Balls

1½ pounds candied cherries, chopped	680 g
½ pound candied pineapple, chopped	228 g
1 (8 ounce) box pitted dates, chopped	1 (228 g)
½ cup flaked coconut	125 ml
4 cups chopped pecans	1 L
1 (14 ounce) can sweetened condensed milk	1 (420 g)

1. Preheat oven to 300° (149° C). In mixing bowl with spoon, combine cherries, pineapple and dates and mix well. Add coconut and pecans and stir. Pour sweetened condensed milk over mixture and mix well.

2. Into miniature paper baking cups, drop mixture by teaspoonfuls and set on baking sheet. Bake 20 to 25 minutes. Store in covered container. Makes 150 to 200 fruit balls.

Lemonade Treats

1 cup shortening	250 ml
1¼ cups sugar	310 ml
2 eggs, well beaten	2
3 cups flour	750 ml
1 teaspoon baking soda	5 ml
½ teaspoon salt	2 ml
1 (6 ounce) can lemonade concentrate, thawed, divided	1 (170 g)
½ teaspoon lemon extract	2 ml
Extra sugar	

1. Preheat oven to 350° (176° C).

2. In mixing bowl with electric mixer, cream shortening and sugar and beat in eggs.

3. Combine flour, baking soda and salt. Add alternately with half lemonade concentrate to shortening mixture and mix well.

4. On greased baking sheet, drop dough by teaspoonfuls and bake 12 to 15 minutes. (Cookies do not need to brown.)

5. Before removing from baking sheet, brush tops of cookies with remaining lemonade concentrate.

6. Sprinkle with sugar and remove from baking sheet to cool.

Lemons on a Sugar Cloud

2 cups (4 sticks) butter, softened	500 ml
1½ cups powdered sugar	375 ml
2 cups flour	500 ml
1¼ cups unsifted corn starch	310 ml
½ teaspoon lemon juice	2 ml

Frosting:

6 tablespoons butter, softened	90 ml
1 (16 ounce) package powdered sugar	1 (454 g)
Lemon juice	

1. Preheat oven to 350° (176° C).

2. In mixing bowl, cream butter and powdered sugar and beat well.

3. Sift flour and corn starch into creamed mixture, add lemon juice and mix well.

4. On ungreased baking sheet, drop dough by teaspoonfuls about 1-inch (2.5 cm) apart and bake 12 to 15 minutes. (Cookies do not need to brown.) Cool.

5. To make frosting, combine butter and powdered sugar and mix in lemon juice a little at a time until frosting reaches spreading consistency. Frost cookies and serve.

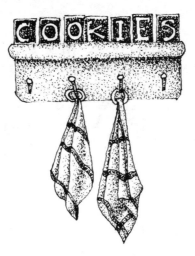

Lemon Cookies

½ (8 ounce) carton frozen whipped topping, softened	½ (228 g)
1 (18 ounce) package lemon cake mix	1 (520 g)
1 egg	1
Powdered sugar	

1. Preheat oven to 350° (176° C). With spoon, stir whipped topping into lemon cake mix. Add egg and mix thoroughly.   Shape into balls and roll in powdered sugar. Bake 8 to 10 minutes. Do not overcook.

Lemon Drops

1 cup (2 sticks) butter, softened	250 ml
1 cup oil	250 ml
1½ cups sugar	375 ml
1½ cups powdered sugar	375 ml
2 teaspoons lemon extract	10 ml
2 eggs	2
4 cups flour	1 L
1 teaspoon cream of tartar	5 ml
½ teaspoon salt	2 ml
1 teaspoon baking soda	5 ml

1. Preheat oven to 350° (176° C). In mixing bowl, combine butter, oil and both sugars and mix well. Add lemon extract and eggs and beat 1 minute. In separate bowl, combine flour, cream of tartar, salt and baking soda. Fold dry ingredients into butter-sugar mixture and mix well. On ungreased baking sheet, drop dough by teaspoonfuls and bake 10 to 11 minutes. (Cookies do not need to brown.)

Pineapple Drops

1 cup shortening	250 ml
2 cups packed brown sugar	500 ml
½ cup sugar	125 ml
2 eggs	2
1 (15 ounce) can crushed pineapple, well drained	1 (438 g)
4 cups flour	1 L
½ teaspoon baking powder	2 ml
2 teaspoons vanilla	10 ml
1 cup chopped pecans	250 ml

1. Preheat oven to 375° (190° C).

2. In mixing bowl, beat shortening, both sugars and eggs. Add very dry pineapple and stir.

3. In separate bowl, combine flour and baking powder. Add to shortening-sugar mixture and mix well.

4. Fold in vanilla and pecans and mix well.

5. On greased baking sheet, drop dough by teaspoonfuls and bake about 12 minutes.

6. Cool before storing.

Orange Crispies

1 (18 ounce) package white cake mix	1 (520 g)
½ cup (1 stick) butter, melted	125 ml
1 egg, beaten	1
2 teaspoons orange extract	10 ml
1 tablespoon orange zest	15 ml
1 cup rice crispy cereal	250 ml
⅔ cup slivered almonds	160 ml

1. Preheat oven to 350° (176° C). In mixing bowl, combine cake mix, melted butter, egg, orange extract and orange peel and mix by hand. Stir in rice crispies and almonds.

2. Roll into 1-inch (2.5 cm) balls and place 2 inches (5 cm) apart on ungreased cookie sheet. Bake for 13 to 14 minutes or until lightly brown. Cool.

Candied Fruit Cookies

1 (16 ounce) package mixed candied fruit	1 (454 g)
½ cup flour	125 ml
1 (3 ounce) can flaked coconut	1 (85 g)
2 cups chopped pecans	500 ml
1 (14 ounce) can sweetened condensed milk	1 (420 g)

1. Preheat oven to 275° (135° C). Dredge candied fruit in flour. (Make sure all flour is used.) In medium bowl, add coconut and pecans and mix well. Stir in condensed milk and mix thoroughly.

2. On greased baking sheet, drop dough by spoonfuls and bake 25 to 28 minutes. Cool and store in airtight container about 5 days before serving.

Frosted Orange Drops

2 cups sugar	500 ml
1 cup (2 sticks) butter, softened	250 ml
2 eggs	2
½ cup orange juice	125 ml
1 cup sour cream	250 ml
1 teaspoon vanilla	5 ml
4½ cups flour	1 L + 125 ml
1 teaspoon baking powder	5 ml
½ teaspoon salt	2 ml

Frosting:

1 cup powdered sugar	250 ml
3 tablespoons butter, softened	45 ml
2 tablespoons orange juice	30 ml
½ teaspoon orange extract	2 ml
1 drop yellow food coloring, optional	1

1. Preheat oven to 350° (176° C).

2. In large mixing bowl, combine sugar, butter, eggs, orange juice, sour cream and vanilla and mix well.

3. Add flour, baking powder and salt and mix well.

3. On greased baking sheet, drop dough by teaspoonfuls 1 inch apart and bake 13 to 15 minutes. (Do not overbake. Cookies will not brown.) Cool.

4. To make frosting, mix all frosting ingredients until very smooth. Frost cookies.

Orange-Nut Drops

½ cup (1 stick) butter, softened	125 ml
1 (3 ounce) package cream cheese, softened	1 (85 g)
¾ cup sugar	180 ml
1 egg, beaten	1
1 teaspoon orange extract	5 ml
1 tablespoon orange zest	15 ml
1 cup flour	250 ml
1 tablespoon salt	15 ml
¾ cup chopped walnuts	180 ml

1. Preheat oven to 350° (176° C).

2. In mixing bowl, cream butter, cream cheese and sugar and beat until creamy. Add egg, orange extract and orange zest and mix well.

3. Fold in flour and salt and mix well. Stir in walnuts.

4. On lightly greased baking sheet, drop dough by teaspoonfuls and bake 12 to 15 minutes or until cookies brown slightly.

5. Cool before storing.

Classic Orange-Slice Cookies

1 cup sugar	250 ml
1 cup packed brown sugar	250 ml
⅔ cup shortening	160 ml
3 eggs, beaten	3
2 cups flour	500 ml
½ teaspoon baking soda	2 ml
½ teaspoon baking powder	2 ml
¼ teaspoon salt	1 ml
½ pound candied orange slices, chopped	228 g
1 cup chopped pecans	250 ml

1. Preheat oven to 350° (176° C).

2. In mixing bowl, combine sugar, brown sugar and shortening and mix well. Add eggs and beat well.

3. In separate bowl, combine flour, baking soda, baking powder and salt. Add to sugar-shortening mixture and mix well.

4. Fold in orange slices and pecans. (The best way to chop orange slices is to cut them with kitchen scissors.)

5. On greased baking sheet, drop dough by teaspoonfuls and bake 14 to 15 minutes.

6. Cool before storing.

Orange-Dream Cookies

1 cup (2 sticks) butter, softened	250 ml
¾ cup sugar	180 ml
½ cup packed light brown sugar	125 ml
1 egg	1
2 tablespoons orange juice	30 ml
2 tablespoons orange peel	30 ml
1 teaspoon orange extract	5 ml
2¼ cups flour	560 ml
¾ teaspoon baking soda	4 ml
½ teaspoon salt	2 ml
1 (12 ounce) package white chocolate morsels	1 (340 g)

1. Preheat oven to 350° (176° C).

2. In mixing bowl, combine butter, both sugars, egg and orange juice and beat well. Add orange peel, orange extract, flour, baking soda and salt and mix well.

3. On ungreased baking sheets, drop dough by rounded tablespoonfuls and bake 12 minutes or until edges turn light golden brown.

4. Let stand on baking sheet about 2 minutes before removing cookies.

5. Cool to room temperature before storing.

Frosted-Pineapple Cookies

1½ cups sugar	375 ml
½ cup packed brown sugar	125 ml
1 cup shortening	250 ml
2 eggs, beaten	2
1 (15 ounce) can crushed pineapple, well drained	1 (438 g)
1 teaspoon vanilla	5 ml
4 cups flour	1 L
1 teaspoon baking soda	5 ml
⅛ teaspoon salt	.5 ml

Frosting:

¼ cup (½ stick) butter	60 ml
¼ cup boiling water	60 ml
¾ teaspoon almond flavoring	4 ml
1 (16 ounce) box powdered sugar	1 (454 g)

1. Preheat oven to 350° (176° C).

2. In mixing bowl, combine and beat both sugars and shortening. Add eggs and mix well.

3. Stir in pineapple and vanilla and mix well. Stir in flour, baking soda and salt and mix well.

4. On baking sheet, drop dough by teaspoonfuls and bake about 10 minutes or until cookies brown slightly.

5. To make frosting, heat butter and water in saucepan until butter melts.

6. Remove from heat and stir in almond flavoring and powdered sugar. Frost cookies.

Party-Pineapple Cookies

1 cup (2 sticks) butter, softened	250 ml
1 cup sugar	250 ml
1 cup packed brown sugar	250 ml
2 eggs	2
1 (15 ounce) can crushed pineapple, juice reserved	1 (438 g)
2 teaspoons vanilla	10 ml
4 cups flour	1 L
1 teaspoon baking powder	5 ml
1 cup chopped pecans	250 ml

Frosting:

2 cups powdered sugar	500 ml
1 tablespoon butter, softened	15 ml
2 to 3 tablespoons pineapple juice	30 to 45 ml
3 drops yellow food coloring	3

1. Preheat oven to 350° (176° C).

2. In mixing bowl, cream butter, both sugars and eggs and beat well.

3. Add pineapple, vanilla, flour and baking powder and mix well. Stir in pecans.

4. On greased baking sheet, drop dough by teaspoonfuls and bake 12 to 14 minutes. Cool.

5. To make frosting, mix all ingredients with just enough pineapple juice to make good spreading consistency.

6. Frost cookies and store in covered container.

Iced-Pumpkin Drops

⅓ cup shortening	80 ml
1½ cups sugar	375 ml
½ (15 ounce) can pumpkin	½ (438 g)
1 egg	1
¼ cup milk	60 ml
3 cups flour	750 ml
1 teaspoon baking soda	5 ml
1 teaspoon ground cinnamon	5 ml
½ teaspoon allspice	2 ml

Cinnamon icing:

¼ cup (½ stick) butter, softened	125 ml
1½ cups powdered sugar	375 ml
About 1 tablespoon milk	15 ml
⅔ teaspoon ground cinnamon	3 ml
½ teaspoon vanilla	2 ml

1. Preheat over to 350° (176° C).

2. In mixing bowl, cream shortening and sugar. Beat in pumpkin, egg and milk.

3. Stir in flour, baking soda, cinnamon and allspice and mix well.

4. Drop by tablespoonfuls onto greased cookie sheet. Bake for 10 to 12 minutes or until light brown. Cool completely.

5. For icing, stir butter and powdered sugar. Add just enough milk to make mixture spreadable.

6. Add cinnamon and vanilla and beat until creamy. Ice cookies when they are cool.

Classic Mincemeat Cookies

1 cup (2 sticks) butter, softened	250 ml
1⅔ cups sugar	410 ml
3 eggs, beaten	3
1 teaspoon baking soda	5 ml
2 teaspoons hot water	10 ml
½ teaspoon salt	2 ml
3¼ cups flour	810 ml
1¼ cups chopped pecans	310 ml
1 cup prepared mincemeat	250 ml

1. Preheat oven to 350° (176° C).

2. In mixing bowl, cream butter and add sugar gradually. Add eggs and mix well.

3. Dissolve baking soda in hot water and pour into butter mixture. Mix well.

4. Add salt and flour and mix well. Stir in pecans and mincemeat.

5. On baking sheets, drop dough by teaspoonfuls and bake 14 to 15 minutes or until cookies begin to brown.

If you haven't tried mincemeat, you don't know what you're missing! Give this recipe a try.

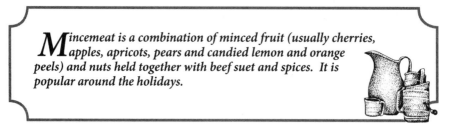

Mincemeat is a combination of minced fruit (usually cherries, apples, apricots, pears and candied lemon and orange peels) and nuts held together with beef suet and spices. It is popular around the holidays.

Classic Fruit Cookies

1 (16 ounce) package red candied cherries, chopped	1 (454 g)
1 (16 ounce) package green candied pineapple, chopped	1 (454 g)
1 pound chopped pecans	454 g
3 cups flour, divided	750 ml
1 teaspoon baking soda	5 ml
1 teaspoon ground cinnamon	5 ml
1 teaspoon ground nutmeg	5 ml
½ teaspoon ground cloves	2 ml
½ cup (1 stick) butter, softened	125 ml
1 cup firmly packed brown sugar	250 ml
4 eggs	4
½ cup bourbon	125 ml
¼ cup milk	60 ml

1. Preheat oven to 300° (149° C).

2. In large bowl, combine cherries, pineapple, pecans and ½ cup (125 ml) flour. Toss to coat fruit and set aside.

3. Combine remaining flour with baking soda, cinnamon, nutmeg and cloves and set aside.

4. In mixing bowl, beat butter and brown sugar until fluffy. Add eggs and beat well.

5. Stir in dry ingredients, bourbon and milk and mix well. Stir in fruit mixture.

6. On lightly greased baking sheet, drop dough by teaspoonfuls and bake about 20 minutes. Cool.

Holiday Fruit Cookies

1 cup (2 sticks) butter, softened	250 ml
¾ cup sugar	180 ml
1 cup packed brown sugar	250 ml
1 teaspoon vanilla	5 ml
2 eggs	2
2½ cups flour	625 ml
1 teaspoon baking soda	5 ml
½ teaspoon salt	2 ml
1 (12 ounce) package white chocolate chips	1(340 g)
1 cup chopped pecans	250 ml
1 (3½ ounce) can flaked coconut	1(85 g)
20 red candied cherries, chopped	20
20 green candied cherries, chopped	20

1. Preheat oven to 350°(176° C).

2. In mixing bowl, cream butter, both sugars, vanilla and eggs and beat well.

3. In separate bowl, combine flour, baking soda and salt. Gradually add to sugar mixture and mix well. Stir in remaining ingredients.

4. On ungreased baking sheet, drop dough by teaspoonfuls and bake for 8 to 10 minutes. Cool before storing.

Coconut Crunchies

1 cup sugar	250 ml
1 cup packed brown sugar	250 ml
1 cup shortening	250 ml
2 eggs	2
1 teaspoon vanilla	5 ml
2 cups flour	500 ml
½ teaspoon baking powder	2 ml
1 teaspoon baking soda	5 ml
½ teaspoon salt	2 ml
2 cups oats	500 ml
2 cups corn flakes	500 ml
1 cup flaked coconut	250 ml

1. Preheat oven to 350° (176° C).

2. In mixing bowl, cream both sugars, shortening, eggs and vanilla and mix well.

3. In separate bowl, combine remaining ingredients. Stir into sugar-shortening mixture and mix well.

4. On greased baking sheet, drop dough by teaspoonfuls and bake 10 minutes or until cookies brown lightly.

5. Cool before storing.

Classic Coconut Macaroons

2 egg whites	2
½ teaspoon salt	2 ml
¼ teaspoon almond extract	1 ml
1 cup sugar	250 ml
1 cup shredded coconut	250 ml
1 cup corn flakes, crushed lightly	250 ml

1. Preheat oven to 350° (176° C). Beat egg whites until stiff and add salt and almond extract.

2. Gradually beat in sugar. Fold in coconut and cornflakes. Drop from teaspoon on greased baking sheet.

3. Bake for about 20 minutes or until light brown on top. Remove from pan with spatula.

The macaroon is well-known internationally and plays an important role in the religious celebrations of many cultures. Macaroons are light and chewy cookies made with egg whites, almonds or coconut and sugar. Jewish Passover meals often include macaroons because they contain no yeast. Though macaroons are available in many different flavors and textures, macaroons are most often characterized by their crisp outside and chewy center.

Angel Macaroons

1 (16 ounce) package 1-step angel food cake mix	1(454 g)
½ cup water	125 ml
1½ teaspoons almond extract	7 ml
2 cups flaked coconut	500 ml

1. Preheat oven to 350° (176° C).

2. In mixing bowl with electric mixer on low speed, beat cake mix, water and extract 30 seconds.

3. Scrape bowl and beat on medium speed 1 minute. Fold in coconut.

4. On parchment paper-lined baking sheet, drop dough by rounded teaspoonfuls and bake 10 to 12 minutes or until cookies set.

5. Remove parchment paper with cookies to wire rack to cool. Store in airtight container.

Chocolate Macaroons

1 (4 ounce) package sweet baking chocolate	1(115 g)
2 egg whites, room temperature	2
½ cup sugar	125 ml
¼ teaspoon salt	1 ml
¼ teaspoon vanilla	1 ml
1 (7 ounce) can flaked coconut	1(198 g)

1. Preheat oven to 350° (176° C).

2. In top of double boiler, stir and melt chocolate. Remove from heat and cool.

3. In small mixing bowl with electric mixer, beat egg whites at high speed for 1 minute. Gradually add sugar 1 tablespoon (15 ml) at a time, and beat until stiff peaks form (about 3 minutes).

4. Add salt, chocolate and vanilla and beat well. Stir in coconut.

5. On baking sheet lined with brown paper, drop dough by teaspoonfuls and bake 12 to 15 minutes.

6. Transfer cookies to cooling rack.

When eggs are called for in a recipe, use large eggs. Most recipes are based on large eggs.

A Different Macaroon

1 (14 ounce) can sweetened condensed milk	1 (420 g)
2 cups flaked coconut	500 ml
1 (8 ounce) box pitted, chopped dates	1 (228 g)
2½ cups chopped pecans	625 ml
1 teaspoon vanilla	5 ml

1. Preheat oven to 325° (163° C). In large bowl, combine all ingredients and mix well.

2. On sprayed baking sheet, drop dough by spoonfuls and bake 15 to 20 minutes. (Cookies may spread out, so reshape halfway through cooking time if necessary.)

3. Place cookies on wax paper while warm. Cool and store in airtight container.

Party Kisses

3 egg whites	3
1 cup sugar	250 ml
2 teaspoons vanilla	10 ml
½ teaspoon almond extract	2 ml
3⅓ cups frosted flakes cereal	830 ml
1 cup chopped pecans	250 ml

1. Preheat oven to 250° (121° C). In mixing bowl, beat egg whites until stiff. Gradually add sugar, vanilla and almond extract.

2. Fold in cereal and pecans. On baking sheet lined with parchment paper, drop dough by teaspoonfuls and bake 40 minutes.

Butterscotch Cookies

1 cup (2 sticks) butter, softened	250 ml
¾ cup packed brown sugar	180 ml
¾ cup sugar	180 ml
2 eggs	2
2 teaspoons vanilla	10 ml
3 cups flour	750 ml
1 teaspoon baking soda	5 ml
½ teaspoon salt	2 ml
¼ teaspoon cinnamon	1 ml
1 (12 ounce) package butterscotch morsels	1(340 g)

1. Preheat oven to 350° (176° C).

2. In large mixing bowl, cream butter and both sugars. Add eggs and vanilla.

3. In separate bowl, combine flour, baking soda, salt and cinnamon and gradually add to sugar mixture. Stir in butterscotch morsels.

4. On ungreased baking sheet, drop dough by teaspoonfuls and bake 10 to 15 minutes or until cookies brown lightly.

Butterscotch flavoring was developed in 1817.

Favorite Butterscotch Cookies

2¼ cups flour	560 ml
1 teaspoon baking soda	5 ml
1 teaspoon salt	5 ml
1 cup (2 sticks) butter, softened	250 ml
½ cup sugar	125 ml
1 cup packed brown sugar	250 ml
1½ teaspoons rum flavoring	7 ml
2 eggs	2
1 (12 ounce) package butterscotch chips	1(340 g)
1 cup chopped pecans or walnuts	250 ml

1. Preheat oven to 350° (176° C).

2. In small bowl, combine flour, baking soda and salt and set aside.

3. In mixing bowl, combine butter, both sugars and rum flavoring and beat until creamy. Beat in eggs.

4. Gradually add flour mixture and mix well. Fold in butterscotch chips and pecans.

5. On ungreased baking sheet, drop dough by tablespoonfuls and bake 10 to 11 minutes.

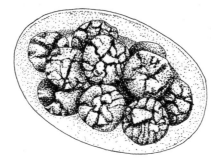

Butterscotch-Pecan Cookies

½ cup (1 stick) butter, softened	125 ml
1 cup sugar	250 ml
1 egg	1
½ teaspoon vanilla	2 ml
1½ cups flour	375 ml
½ teaspoon baking powder	2 ml
½ teaspoon baking soda	2 ml
½ teaspoon salt	2 ml
1 (6 ounce) package butterscotch morsels, chopped	1(170 g)
1¼ cups chopped pecans	310 ml

1. Preheat oven to 350° (176° C).

2. In large mixing bowl, cream butter, sugar, egg and vanilla.

3. In separate bowl, combine flour, baking powder, baking soda and salt and gradually add to sugar mixture.

4. Stir in butterscotch morsels (chopped in food processor, if desired) and pecans.

5. On ungreased baking sheet, drop dough by teaspoonfuls and bake 12 to 15 minutes.

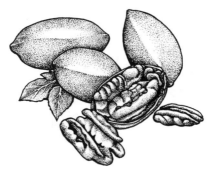

Peanut-Butterscotch Cookies

½ cup (1 stick) butter, softened	125 ml
½ cup crunchy peanut butter	125 ml
½ cup sugar	125 ml
¾ cup packed light brown sugar	180 ml
1 egg	1
1 teaspoon vanilla	5 ml
1 tablespoon milk	15 ml
1¾ cups flour	430 ml
½ teaspoon baking soda	2 ml
½ teaspoon salt	2 ml
1 (6 ounce) package butterscotch chips	1(170 g)

1. Preheat oven to 350° (176° C).

2. In mixing bowl, cream butter, peanut butter, both sugars, egg, vanilla and milk and beat well.

3. Add flour, baking soda and salt and mix well. Stir in butterscotch chips.

4. Place 1 teaspoonful (5 cm) dough on greased baking sheet. Bake about 12 minutes or until edges turn light golden brown.

5. Remove from oven and let stand 2 or 3 minutes before removing cookies.

6. Cool before storing.

Butterscotch Crisp

1 cup oil	250 ml
2 eggs, beaten	2
1 cup packed light brown sugar	250 ml
1 cup sugar	250 ml
1 teaspoon vanilla	5 ml
¾ cup chopped pecans	180 ml
1 (6 ounce) package butterscotch chips	1(170 g)
2 cups flour	500 ml
1 cup oats	250 ml
½ teaspoon baking powder	2 ml
½ teaspoon baking soda	2 ml
½ teaspoon salt	2 ml
2 cups corn flakes	500 ml

1. Preheat oven to 325° (163° C).

2. In large bowl, combine all ingredients except corn flakes. After ingredients mix well, gently stir in corn flakes.

3. On ungreased baking sheet, drop mixture by spoonfuls and bake 8 to 10 minutes. Remove from pan to cool.

Butterscotch Meringues

2 egg whites	2
⅛ teaspoon salt	.5 ml
⅛ teaspoon cream of tartar	.5 ml
1 teaspoon vanilla	5 ml
1 cup sugar	250 ml
1 (6 ounce) package butterscotch chips	1(170 g)
¾ cup finely chopped pecans	180 ml

1. Preheat oven to 300° (149°).

2. In mixing bowl, beat egg whites to thicken. Add salt, cream of tartar and vanilla and continue beating until soft peaks form.

3. Gradually spoon in sugar and beat until peaks are stiff. Fold in butterscotch chips and pecans.

4. Cover baking sheet with parchment paper and drop cookies by rounded teaspoonfuls. Bake 25 minutes.

5. Remove cookies from oven, let stand 2 to 3 minutes and transfer to cooling rack.

Butter Brickle Crunch

½ cup (1 stick) butter, softened	125 ml
1 cup packed light brown sugar	250 ml
1 egg	1
1 teaspoon vanilla	5 ml
1½ cups flour	375 ml
½ teaspoon baking soda	2 ml
½ teaspoon salt	2 ml
1 (7.8 ounce) package butter brickle chips	1 (210 g)
½ cup chopped pecans	125 ml

1. Preheat oven to 350° (176° C).

2. In mixing bowl, blend butter, brown sugar, egg and vanilla until smooth and creamy.

3. In separate bowl, combine flour, baking soda and salt. Stir dry ingredients into creamed mixture and mix well.

4. Fold in butter brickles and chopped pecans.

5. On greased baking sheet, drop dough by tablespoonfuls 2 inches (5 cm) apart and bake 13 to 14 minutes. Remove from baking sheet and cool.

Ginger Gems

½ cup (1 stick) butter, softened	125 ml
¾ cup sugar	180 ml
1 egg	1
1 tablespoon lemon juice	15 ml
1⅔ cups flour	410 ml
½ teaspoon baking soda	2 ml
½ cup finely chopped crystallized ginger	125 ml

1. Preheat oven to 350° (176° C). In mixing bowl with electric mixer, beat butter, sugar, egg and lemon juice 3 to 4 minutes.

2. With mixer at low speed, gradually add flour and soda. Beat another 3 to 4 minutes and fold in crystallized ginger.

3. On well greased baking sheet, drop dough by teaspoonfuls and bake 13 to 15 minutes or until cookies turn golden, but not brown.

Yummy Cookies

3 egg whites	3
1¼ cups sugar	310 ml
2 teaspoons vanilla	10 ml
3½ cups frosted flakes cereal	875 ml
1 cup chopped pecans	250 ml

1. Preheat oven to 350° (176° C).

2. In mixing bowl, beat egg whited until stiff. Gradually add sugar and vanilla.

3. Fold in frosted flakes and pecans. On baking sheet, drop dough by teaspoonfuls and bake 30 minutes.

Classic Shortbread Cookies

2 cups (4 sticks) butter, softened	**500 ml**
1 cup powdered sugar	**250 ml**
4 cups flour	**1 L**
Additional powdered sugar	

1. Preheat oven to 350° (176° C). Cream butter until light and fluffy. Gradually add sugar and beat vigorously after each addition until sugar completely dissolves.

2. Add flour, a little at a time, beating well after each addition. Chill dough for 1 hour.

3. Sprinkle surface with equal parts of flour and powdered sugar and turn one third of dough at a time onto surface.

4. Pat into thickness of ½ inch (1.5 cm) and cut cookies with 1½-inch (3.5 cm) biscuit cutter. Place on ungreased cookie sheet and prick tops of cookies with fork to make a design.

5. Bake 15 to 20 minutes or until light golden color. Remove from oven and cool slightly before dusting lightly with powdered sugar.

Simply Good Shortbread

2 cups (4 sticks) butter, softened	**500 ml**
1½ cups packed light brown sugar	**375 ml**
4 cups flour	**1 L**

1. Preheat oven to 250° (121° C). In mixing bowl, mix all ingredients.

2. In greased 9 x 13-inch (23 x 33 cm) baking dish, pat dough and bake 1 hour. Increase temperature to 300° (149° C) and bake additional 15 minutes.

3. While shortbread is still warm, cut in small squares, but do not remove from pan until cool.

Be sure to use butter. There is no substitute
for the real thing in this recipe.

Classic Scotch Shortbread

1 cup (2 sticks) butter	**250 ml**
2 cups flour	**500 ml**
¾ cup corn starch	**180 ml**
⅔ cup sugar	**160 ml**
Colored sprinkles or sugar	

1. Preheat oven to 325° (163° C). In saucepan, melt butter and stir in flour, corn starch and sugar.

2. In 9-inch (23 cm) square pan, press dough and bake 45 minutes.

3. Cut in squares immediately after removing from oven.

4. Sprinkle with colored sugar sprinkles or granulated sugar.

Shortbread Crunchies

1 cup (2 sticks) butter	250 ml
1 cup oil	250 ml
1 cup sugar	250 ml
1 cup packed brown sugar	250 ml
1 egg	1
1 teaspoon vanilla	5 ml
1 cup quick-cooking oats	250 ml
3½ cups sifted flour	875 ml
1 teaspoon baking soda	5 ml
1 teaspoon salt	5 ml
1 cup crushed corn flakes	250 ml
1 (3½ ounce) can flaked coconut	1(95 g)
1 cup chopped pecans	250 ml

1. Preheat oven to 325° (163° C).

2. In mixing bowl, cream butter, oil and both sugars. Add egg and vanilla and mix well.

3. Stir in oats, flour, baking soda and salt. Add corn flakes, coconut and pecans and mix.

4. On ungreased baking sheet, drop dough by teaspoonfuls and flatten with spoon dipped in water. Prick cookies with fork to make design.

5. Bake 15 minutes or until cookies brown slightly.

Vanishing Butter Cookies

1 (18 ounce) package butter cake mix	1(520 g)
1 (3.4 ounce) package instant butterscotch pudding mix	1(95 g)
1 cup oil	250 ml
1 egg, beaten	1
1¼ cups chopped pecans	225 ml

1. Preheat oven to 350° (176° C).

2. In mixing bowl with spoon, mix cake mix and dry pudding mix. Stir in oil.

3. Add egg and mix thoroughly. Stir in pecans.

4. With teaspoon or small cookie scoop, place cookie dough on baking sheet about 2 inches (5 cm) apart.

5. Bake 8 to 9 minutes. Do not overcook.

There is no substitute for butter in baking. Margarine, light and whipped butter contain water and do not contain enough fat for baking.

Frosted Butter Cookies

1 cup (2 sticks) butter, softened	250 ml
½ cup powdered sugar, sifted	125 ml
¾ cup corn starch, sifted	180 ml
1 cup flour	250 ml

Frosting:

1 (3 ounce) package cream cheese, softened	1 (85 g)
1⅔ cups powdered sugar	410 ml
1 teaspoon vanilla	5 ml

1. Preheat oven to 350° (176° C).

2. In mixing bowl, beat butter until creamy. Add powdered sugar, corn starch and flour and mix until batter becomes stiff.

3. On greased baking sheet, drop dough by teaspoonfuls and bake 10 to 12 minutes. (Watch closely because cookies do not need to brown.)

4. Make frosting while cookies are baking so you can frost warm cookies.

5. In mixing bowl with electric mixer, beat cream cheese, powdered sugar and vanilla.

6. Frost tops of cookies and handle carefully because cookies will be fragile.

Tip: Be sure to use butter. There is no substitute for the real thing in this recipe.

Classic Melting Moments

1 cup butter, softened	250 ml
⅓ cup powdered sugar	80 ml
¾ cup cornstarch	180 ml
1 cup flour	250 ml
2 tablespoons butter, melted	30 ml
1 teaspoon vanilla, lemon or orange extract	5 ml
1 cup powdered sugar	250 ml
Cream	

1. Stir butter until creamy and gradually add powdered sugar. Add cornstarch and flour and mix well. Chill 1 hour.

2. Form into balls and place on ungreased cookie sheet. Bake at 350° (176° C) for about 15 minutes. Set aside to cool.

3. Mix butter, flavoring, powdered sugar and just enough cream to reach spreading consistency. Spread over each cookie.

Irish Cookies

1 cup (2 sticks) butter, softened	250 ml
1 cup sugar	250 ml
2 eggs, beaten	2
1 teaspoon almond extract	5 ml
2 cups flour	500 ml
1 teaspoon cream of tartar	5 ml
½ teaspoon baking soda	2 ml
¼ teaspoon salt	1 ml
¼ teaspoon ground nutmeg	1 ml

Frosting:

3 cups powdered sugar	750 ml
¼ cup (½ stick) butter, softened	60 ml
1 teaspoon almond extract	5 ml
2 to 3 tablespoons warm water	30 to 45 ml
Green food coloring	

1. Preheat oven to 350° (176° C).

2. In mixing bowl, cream butter and sugar until fluffy. Beat in eggs and almond extract.

3. In separate bowl, combine flour, cream of tartar, baking soda, salt and nutmeg and gradually add to creamed mixture.

4. On ungreased baking sheet, drop dough by rounded teaspoonfuls and bake 8 to 10 minutes. Remove from oven and cool on wire racks.

5. To make frosting, combine powdered sugar, butter, almond extract and just enough water to give frosting spreading consistency.

6. Tint with green food coloring and frost cookies.

Honey Dainties

¼ cup oil	60 ml
½ cup (1 stick) butter, softened	125 ml
⅔ cup sugar	160 ml
1 tablespoon orange juice	15 ml
1 teaspoon baking powder	5 ml
½ teaspoon baking soda	2 ml
2 cups flour	500 ml

Syrup:

¾ cup sugar	180 ml
½ cup water	125 ml
⅓ cup honey	80 ml
½ cup very finely chopped pecans	125 ml

1. Preheat oven to 350° (176° C).

2. In mixing bowl, combine and beat oil, butter and sugar. Add orange juice, baking powder, baking soda and flour and mix well.

3. Shape dough in 2-inch (5 cm) balls and place on ungreased baking sheet.

4. Bake about 20 minutes or until cookies turn golden.

5. As cookies bake, combine sugar, water and honey in saucepan. Boil uncovered 4 minutes and cool.

6. Dip face of each cookie in warm syrup and press into chopped pecans.

7. Dry and store in covered container.

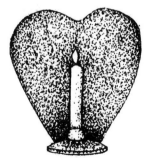

Sesame Balls

2 cups flour	500 ml
1 cup sugar	250 ml
1½ teaspoons baking powder	7 ml
⅛ teaspoon salt	.5 ml
¾ cup shortening	180 ml
2 egg yolks	2
¼ cup milk	60 ml
1 teaspoon almond extract	5 ml
About ⅓ cup sesame seeds	80 ml

1. Preheat oven to 350° (176° C).

2. In large bowl, combine flour, sugar, baking powder and salt. Cut in shortening until mixture resembles coarse crumbs.

3. Add egg yolks, milk and almond extract and mix until dough holds together.

4. Shape dough in 1-inch (2.5 cm) balls, roll in sesame seeds and coat completely. Place on greased baking sheet.

5. Bake 12 to 15 minutes or until cookies brown lightly.

Simple Sesames

1 cup sesame seeds	250 ml
¼ cup shredded coconut	60 ml
¾ cup shortening	180 ml
1 cup packed brown sugar	250 ml
½ cup sugar	125 ml
1 egg	1
1 teaspoon vanilla	5 ml
2 cups flour	500 ml
1 teaspoon baking powder	5 ml
½ teaspoon baking soda	2 ml
½ teaspoon salt	2 ml

1. Toast sesame seeds and coconut at 300° (149°) until they brown lightly.

2. Increase heat to 350° (176° C) to preheat for cookies.

3. In mixing bowl, cream shortening with both sugars. Add egg, vanilla, toasted sesame seeds and coconut.

4. Beat well and add flour, baking powder, baking soda and salt and mix.

5. Use about 1 teaspoon (5 ml) dough for each cookie and shape into small balls.

6. On greased baking sheet, place dough and flatten with fork.

7. Bake at 350° (176° C) for 8 to 10 minutes.

None-Better Cookies

½ cup (1 stick) butter, softened	125 ml
1 cup shortening	250 ml
2 cups sugar	500 ml
2 eggs, beaten	2
2½ tablespoons almond extract	37 ml
3¾ cups flour	930 ml
2½ teaspoons baking soda	12 ml
½ teaspoon salt	2 ml
40 whole almonds	40

1. In mixing bowl, combine butter, shortening and sugar and beat until creamy. Add eggs one at a time and beat well. Add almond extract and mix.

2. In separate bowl, combine flour, baking soda and salt and stir into butter-sugar mixture to make smooth dough. Cover and chill several hours.

3. Form dough in 1½-inch (3 cm) balls and place 2 inches (5 cm) apart on greased baking sheet.

4. Flatten slightly with hand and place a whole almond on each cookie.

5. Bake at 350° (176° C) for 10 to 12 minutes or until cookies brown slightly on bottom, but not on top. Cool.

Coffee and Cookies

1 cup (2 sticks) butter, softened	250 ml
1 cup sugar	250 ml
2 cups finely chopped pecans	500 ml
3 teaspoons flour	15 ml
2 teaspoons vanilla	10 ml
2 teaspoons instant coffee	10 ml
Dash salt	
Powdered sugar	

1. Preheat oven to 325° (163° C).

2. In mixing bowl, cream butter and sugar.

3. In separate bowl, dredge pecans in flour. Add floured pecans to butter-sugar mixture.

4. Fold in vanilla, instant coffee and salt. (Mixture will be very dry.)

5. With tablespoon, scoop dough and roll in 1-inch (2.5 cm) balls.

6. On baking sheet, place dough and bake 16 to 18 minutes. Cool, then roll cookies in powdered sugar.

7. Store in airtight container.

Cinnamon Cookies

1 cup (2 sticks) butter, softened	250 ml
3½ cups sugar	875 ml
4 eggs	4
5½ cups flour	1.25 L
1 teaspoon salt	5 ml
2 teaspoons baking soda	10 ml
4 teaspoons cream of tartar	20 ml
2 teaspoons ground cinnamon	10 ml
¾ cup sugar	180 ml

1. In mixing bowl, combine butter, 3½ cups (875 ml) sugar and eggs and beat until fluffy.

2. In separate bowl, combine flour, salt, baking soda and cream of tartar. Gradually mix dry ingredients into creamed mixture.

3. When thoroughly mixed, cover and chill dough several hours or until dough is completely chilled.

4. In small bowl, combine cinnamon and ¾ cup (180 ml) sugar.

5. Roll chilled dough in 1-inch (2.5 cm) balls and roll each ball in cinnamon-sugar mixture.

6. On ungreased baking sheet, place dough and bake at 350° (176° C) for 8 to 10 minutes or until cookies brown lightly.

Cinnamon-Ginger Cookies

¾ cup shortening	180 ml
1 cup sugar	250 ml
1 egg, beaten	1
¼ cup molasses	60 ml
2 cups flour	500 ml
2 teaspoons baking soda	10 ml
1 teaspoon cinnamon	5 ml
1½ teaspoons ginger	7 ml
Granulated sugar	

1. In mixing bowl, beat shortening, sugar, egg and molasses.

2. Stir in flour, baking soda, cinnamon and ginger and mix well. Cover and chill several hours.

3. Preheat oven to 350° (176° C) .

4. Shape dough into 1-inch (2.5 cm) balls and dip balls in granulated sugar.

5. On greased baking sheet, place dough balls and bake 10 to 11 minutes.

6. Remove from baking sheet immediately to cool.

Classic Gingersnaps

¾ cup packed brown sugar	180 ml
¾ cup butter or shortening	180 ml
¾ cup light molasses	180 ml
1 egg	1
¾ cup flour	180 ml
2 teaspoons baking soda	10 ml
1 teaspoon cinnamon	5 ml
1 teaspoon ginger	5 ml
½ teaspoon cloves	2 ml
¼ teaspoon salt	1 ml
¼ cup sugar	1 ml

1. Mix brown sugar and butter or shortening until smooth and creamy. Pour into mixture molasses and egg and beat well.

2. Combine flour, baking soda, cinnamon, ginger, cloves and salt. Gradually add to butter mixture and stir after each addition. Mix well.

3. Chill overnight or several hours. When ready to cook, preheat oven to 350°.

4. Form dough in 1 to 2-inch (5 cm) balls and roll in sugar. Place 2 inches (2 cm) apart on cookie sheet. Bake for 10 to 12 minutes.

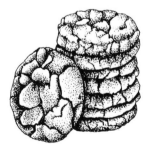

Classic Ginger-Molasses Cookies

1½ cups shortening	375 ml
2¼ cups sugar	560 ml
2 eggs	2
⅔ cup molasses	160 ml
4¼ cups flour	1 L + 60 ml
4 teaspoons baking soda	20 ml
1¼ teaspoons cinnamon	6 ml
1 teaspoon ginger	5 ml
½ teaspoon cloves	2 ml
½ teaspoon salt	2 ml
Extra sugar	

1. In mixing bowl, cream shortening, sugar, eggs and molasses.

2. In separate bowl, combine flour, baking soda, cinnamon, ginger and salt.

3. Add to shortening-molasses mixture and mix well. Chill several hours.

4. Roll dough in 1-inch (2.5 cm) balls. Roll balls in sugar.

5. Bake at 325° (163° C) for about 7 minutes or until cookies just begin to brown.

Molasses played a big role in trade in the American colonies and continued to be America's primary sweetener until after World War I. Molasses was less expensive and more readily available than sugar and was used to sweeten baked goods like pies, cakes, gingerbread, toffee candy and various cookies. Rum was also made from molasses.

Classic Molasses Cookies

1 cup sugar	250 ml
1 cup packed brown sugar	250 ml
1 cup (2 sticks) butter, softened	250 ml
1 egg, beaten	1
3 cups flour	750 ml
1 teaspoon ginger	5 ml
2 teaspoons cinnamon	1 ml
½ teaspoon baking soda	2 ml
½ cup dark molasses	125 ml

1. Preheat oven to 350° (176° C). Mix sugar, brown sugar and butter. Add egg and mix all together.

2. In separate bowl, combine flour, ginger, cinnamon and baking soda. Add flour mixture to sugar-butter mixture in small batches and stir well after each addition.

3. Roll in balls and drop on cookie sheet to bake. If you prefer, roll out dough on wax paper and cut out different shapes with cookie cutters.

4. Bake until slightly firm. Time will vary depending on size of cookies. Watch carefully.

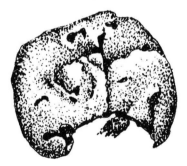

Drop Cookies

1 cup (2 sticks) butter	**250 ml**
2 cups sugar	**500 ml**
2 eggs, beaten	**500 ml**
3 cups buttermilk biscuit baking mix	**750 ml**
2 teaspoons vanilla	**10 ml**
About 50 pecan halves	**50**

1. Preheat oven to 350° (176° C).

2. In mixing bowl, beat butter and sugar until fluffy. Add eggs and beat well.

3. Fold in baking mix and vanilla and beat well.

4. On greased baking sheet, drop dough by tablespoonfuls. Press 1 pecan half into top of each cookie.

5. Bake 6 to 7 minutes and cool before storing.

If a recipe calls for superfine sugar, process granulated sugar in the food processor until the granules become superfine. The finer grain in superfine sugar tends to make cookies have a smoother consistency and less likely to crack during baking.

Classic Sugar Cookies

½ cup butter, softened	125 ml
1 cup sugar	250 ml
1 egg	1
1 tablespoon cream	15 ml
½ teaspoon vanilla	2 ml
1½ cups flour	375 ml
¼ teaspoon salt	1 ml
1 teaspoon baking powder	5 ml

1. Preheat oven to 375° (190° C). Cream butter and slowly add sugar. Beat until light and fluffy.

2. Combine egg, cream and vanilla, add to butter mixture and beat to mix.

3. In a separate bowl, combine flour, baking powder and salt. Add a little flour mixture to butter mixture and mix after each addition.

4. Drop by teaspoon onto greased cookie sheet. Bake for about 8 to 10 minutes. Makes about 5 dozen.

White Sugar Cookies

1 cup sugar	250 ml
1 cup powdered sugar	250 ml
1 cup (2 sticks) butter, softened	250 ml
1 cup oil	250 ml
2 eggs	2
1 tablespoon vanilla	15 ml
1 teaspoon cream of tartar	5 ml
1 teaspoon baking soda	5 ml
4½ cups plus 4 tablespoons flour	1 L + 60 ml
Sugar	

1. In mixing bowl, beat both sugars, butter, oil, eggs and vanilla. Add cream of tartar, baking soda and flour and mix well.

2. Chill several hours or overnight.

3. Preheat oven to 350° (176° C).

4. Shape dough in small balls and place on baking sheet. Dip bottom of glass in water and press down on each cookie to flatten.

5. Bake 8 to 10 minutes. (Do not brown.)

6. Sprinkle sugar on tops of cookies while warm.

Blue Ribbon Sugar Cookies

1 cup sugar	250 ml
½ cup (1 stick) butter, softened	125 ml
½ cup shortening	125 ml
1 egg	1
2 cups flour, sifted	500 ml
½ teaspoon cream of tartar	2 ml
½ teaspoon baking soda	2 ml
⅛ teaspoon salt	.5 ml
1 teaspoon vanilla	5 ml
½ teaspoon almond flavoring	2 ml
Extra butter	
Extra sugar	

1. Preheat oven to 350° (176° C).

2. In mixing bowl, cream sugar, butter and shortening and beat well. Add egg and mix well.

3. In separate bowl, sift flour, cream of tartar, baking soda and salt. Gradually add dry ingredients and flavorings to sugar mixture and mix well.

4. On ungreased baking sheet, drop mixture by teaspoonfuls.

5. On bottom of small glass, spread a little butter and dip glass in sugar. With glass, press down slightly on each cookie. Repeat for each cookie.

6. Bake 10 minutes (cookies should not brown) and cool before storing.

assic Brown Sugar Wafers

ace Blvd.
FL 322C

*(2 sticks) butter, softened	250 ml
¾ cup packed dark brown sugar	180 ml
1 egg yolk	1
1 tablespoon vanilla	15 ml
1¼ cups flour	310 ml

1. In mixing bowl with electric mixer, beat butter and gradually add brown sugar.

2. Add egg yolk and vanilla and beat well. Add flour and dash salt and mix well.

3. Shape dough in 1-inch (2.5 cm) balls and chill 2 hours.

4. On baking sheet, place chilled dough and flatten each ball slightly. Bake at 350° (176°) for 10 to 12 minutes and cool.

Sugar cookies, though always delicious, were once round and plain, with an unassuming dusting of granulated sugar on top. Today they are a favorite of professional and amateur decorators, who cut them into various shapes and decorate with icing, cookie paints and candy. Sugar cookie bouquets are a popular item for showers, parties and other special occasions.

Classic Snickerdoodles

½ cup (1 stick) butter, softened	125 ml
½ cup shortening	125 ml
1½ cups sugar	375 ml
2 eggs	2
2½ cups flour	625 ml
2 teaspoons cream of tartar	10 ml
1 teaspoon baking soda	5 ml
¼ teaspoon salt	1 ml
4 tablespoons sugar	60 ml
2 teaspoons cinnamon	10 ml

1. Preheat oven to 350° (176° C).

2. In medium mixing bowl, mix butter, shortening, 1½ cups (375 ml) sugar and eggs and beat well.

3. Stir in flour, cream of tartar, baking soda and salt.

4. Shape dough by rounded teaspoonfuls into balls.

5. In small bowl, mix 4 tablespoons (60 ml) sugar and cinnamon and roll balls in mixture to cover.

6. On ungreased baking sheet, place balls 2 inches (5 cm) apart and use bottom of jar or glass to mash cookies flat.

7. Bake 8 to 10 minutes or until edges just begin to brown.

Dutch colonial settlers are credited with bringing snickerdoodles to America. The origin of this unusual name is unknown, but snickerdoodles have survived and changed little throughout America's history. Snickerdoodle dough, made with butter, flour, shortening and sometimes spices and/or nuts, is rolled in or sprinkled with cinnamon and sugar before baking. The surface of the cookie often cracks as it rises.

Classic Hermits

½ cup shortening or butter	125 ml
1 cup packed brown sugar	250 r
1 egg	1
½ cups flour	37
½ teaspoon baking soda	2 ml
½ teaspoon cinnamon	2 ml
¼ teaspoon nutmeg	1 ml
¼ teaspoon cloves	1 ml
¼ teaspoon salt	1 ml
2 tablespoons water	30 ml
¾ cup raisins	180 ml
¾ cup chopped walnuts	180 ml

1. Preheat oven to 350° (176° C) . Cream shortening and brown sugar in large bowl. Stir in egg.

2. In separate bowl combine flour, baking soda, cinnamon, nutmeg, cloves and salt. Add flour mixture to brown sugar in small batches and mix well after each addition.

3. Add water, raisins and walnuts and mix well. Drop on baking sheet and bake about 10 minutes until done.

Classic Chewy Oatmeal Cookies

These oatmeal cookies are made with brown sugar and are moist and chewy.

1 cup shortening, softened	250 ml
1 cup brown sugar	250 ml
1 egg, beaten	1
2 teaspoons vanilla	10 ml
⅓ cup milk	80 ml
¾ teaspoon baking soda	4 ml
2 cups flour	500 ml
½ teaspoon salt	2 ml
1 teaspoon cinnamon	5 ml
1 cup golden raisins	250 ml
½ cup chopped pecans	125 ml
2 cups oats	500 ml

1. Preheat oven to 375° (190° C).

2. Cream butter and sugar. Stir in eggs, vanilla and milk and mix well.

3. In separate bowl, combine baking soda, flour, salt and cinnamon.

4. Gradually blend dry ingredients into creamed mixture. Fold in raisins, pecans and oats.

5. On greased baking sheet, drop dough by teaspoonfuls and bake 13 to 14 minutes.

Classic Crispy Oatmeal Cookies

*These oatmeal cookies are made with white sugar
and are crispy with chewy raisins.*

1 cup (2 sticks) butter, softened	**250 ml**
1½ cups sugar	**375 ml**
2 eggs, beaten	**2**
1 tablespoon milk	**15 ml**
¾ teaspoon baking soda	**4 ml**
2 cups flour	**500 ml**
½ teaspoon salt	**2 ml**
1 teaspoon cinnamon	**5 ml**
1 cup golden raisins	**250 ml**
½ cup chopped pecans	**125 ml**
2 cups oats	**500 ml**

1. Preheat oven to 375° (190° C).

2. Cream butter and sugar. Stir in eggs, vanilla and milk and mix well.

3. In separate bowl, combine baking soda, flour, salt and cinnamon.

4. Gradually blend dry ingredients into creamed mixture. Fold in raisins, pecans and oats.

5. On greased baking sheet, drop dough by teaspoonfuls and bake 13 to 14 minutes.

Granny's Ginger-Oat Cookies

½ cup (1 stick) butter, softened	125 ml
¾ cup sugar	180 ml
¾ cup packed brown sugar	180 ml
1 egg	1
1 tablespoon water	15 ml
½ teaspoon vanilla	2 ml
1 cup flour	250 ml
½ teaspoon baking soda	2 ml
½ cup finely chopped crystallized ginger	125 ml
1½ cups quick-cooking oats	375 ml
1 (6 ounce) package chocolate chips	1(170 g)
½ cup chopped pecans	125 ml

1. Preheat oven to 350° (176° C).

2. In mixing bowl, combine butter, both sugars, egg, water and vanilla and beat.

3. Add flour, baking soda and ginger and mix well.

4. Add oats, chocolate chips and pecans and mix well.

5. On baking sheet, drop dough by teaspoonfuls and bake 12 to 15 minutes or until cookies brown.

Old-Fashioned Everyday Oatmeal Cookies

1 cup packed brown sugar	250 ml
1 cup sugar	250 ml
1 cup shortening	250 ml
2 eggs	2
2 tablespoons water	30 ml
2 teaspoons vanilla	10 ml
½ teaspoon salt	2 ml
1 teaspoon baking soda	5 ml
1½ cups flour	375 ml
3 cups quick-cooking oats	750 ml
1 cup chopped pecans	250 ml

1. Preheat oven to 350° (176° C).

2. In mixing bowl, combine both sugars, shortening, eggs, water and vanilla and beat well.

3. Add salt, baking soda and flour and mix. Pour in oats and pecans and mix.

4. On baking sheet, drop dough by teaspoonfuls and bake 14 to 15 minutes.

General Mills had Betty Crocker; Quaker Oats had Mary Alden. In 1943, Quaker introduced "Mary Alden's Favorite Oatmeal Cookie Recipe". The recipe called for shortening, bacon drippings and minimal sugar to compensate for butter and sugar rationing during World War II.

Cocoa-Oatmeal Cookies

1 cup (2 sticks) butter, softened	250 ml
1⅔ cups sugar	410 ml
2 eggs	2
2 teaspoons vanilla	10 ml
¾ teaspoon baking soda	4 ml
½ teaspoon salt	2 ml
1½ cups flour	375 ml
3 tablespoons cocoa	45 ml
1 teaspoon cinnamon	5 ml
2½ cups quick-cooking oats	625 ml
1 cup chopped pecans	250 ml

1. Preheat oven to 350° (176° C).

2. In mixing bowl, cream butter, sugar, eggs and vanilla.

3. In separate bowl, combine baking soda, salt, flour, cocoa and cinnamon and gradually add to sugar mixture. Stir in oats and pecans.

4. On ungreased baking sheet, drop dough by teaspoonfuls and bake 15 to 18 minutes.

Spiced-Oatmeal Cookies

1 cup sugar	250 ml
1 cup packed brown sugar	250 ml
1 cup shortening	250 ml
2 eggs	2
1¾ cups flour	430 ml
1 teaspoon baking powder	5 ml
1 teaspoon baking soda	5 ml
½ teaspoon cinnamon	2 ml
¼ teaspoon nutmeg	1 ml
1½ cups oats	375 ml
1 cup chopped pecans	250 ml
2 teaspoons vanilla	10 ml

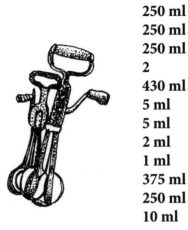

1. Preheat oven to 350° (176° C).

2. In mixing bowl, cream both sugars, shortening and eggs and beat well. Add remaining ingredients and mix.

3. Roll dough in 1-inch (2.5 cm) balls and place on ungreased baking sheet. Bake 10 to 12 minutes.

The Quaker Company is the largest producer of oats in America. In 1997 the company received the first food-specific benefit claim by the FDA confirming that oats reduce heart disease.

Oatmeal Crisps

½ cup (1 stick) butter	125 ml
½ cup packed brown sugar	125 ml
½ cup sugar	125 ml
1 egg	1
1 cup flour	250 ml
1 teaspoon baking soda	5 ml
½ teaspoon salt	2 ml
1 cup quick-cooking oats	250 ml
1 cup crispy rice cereal	250 ml
1 cup flaked coconut	250 ml
1 teaspoon vanilla	5 ml

1. Preheat over to 350° (176° C).

2. In mixing bowl, cream both sugars and egg and beat well.

3. Stir in remaining ingredients and mix well.

4. Roll dough in 1-inch (2.5 cm) balls and place on greased baking sheet.

5. Bake 10 to 15 minutes or until cookies turn golden brown.

The Quaker Oats package was originally square. The familiar round package was introduced in 1915.

Banana-Oatmeal Cookies

1 cup (2 sticks) butter, softened	250 ml
1 cup sugar	250 ml
1 cup packed brown sugar	250 ml
2 eggs	2
1 cup (2 to 3 whole) mashed bananas	250 ml
2 teaspoons vanilla	10 ml
2 cups oats	500 ml
2 cups flour	500 ml
1 teaspoon baking powder	5 ml
1 cup chopped pecans	250 ml
Powdered sugar	

1. Preheat oven to 350° (176° C).

2. In mixing bowl, cream butter, both sugars and eggs and beat well.

3. Add bananas, vanilla, oats, flour and baking powder and mix well. Stir in pecans.

4. On greased baking sheet, drop dough by teaspoonfuls and bake 12 to 14 minutes.

5. Sprinkle sifted powdered sugar over warm cookies. Cool.

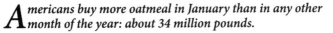

*A*mericans buy more oatmeal in January than in any other month of the year: about 34 million pounds.

Oatmeal Chippers

1 cup (2 sticks) butter, softened	250 ml
½ cup packed brown sugar	125 ml
1 cup sugar	250 ml
2 eggs, beaten	2
2 teaspoons vanilla	10 ml
1½ cups flour	375 ml
1 teaspoon baking soda	5 ml
1 teaspoon salt	5 ml
1 cup chopped walnuts	250 ml
2 cups oats	500 ml
1 (12 ounce) package butterscotch chips	1 (340 g)

1. Preheat oven to 350° (176° C).

2. In mixing bowl, combine butter and both sugars and beat until creamy. Beat in eggs and vanilla.

3. In separate bowl, combine flour, baking soda and salt.

4. Add dry ingredients to butter-sugar mixture and blend well. Stir in walnuts, oats and butterscotch chips.

5. On greased baking sheet, drop dough by tablespoonfuls and bake 12 to 14 minutes or until cookies brown slightly. Cool before storing.

Peanutty Oatmeal Cookies

½ cup (1 stick) butter, softened	125 ml
2 cups sugar	500 ml
1½ cups packed brown sugar	375 ml
4 eggs, beaten	4
1 teaspoon vanilla	5 ml
1 (16 ounce) jar chunky peanut butter	1(454 g)
6 cups oats	1.5 L
2½ teaspoons baking soda	12 ml
1 (6 ounce) package butterscotch chips	1(170 g)

1. Preheat oven to 350° (176° C).

2. In mixing bowl with electric mixer, beat butter, both sugars, eggs and vanilla on low speed until smooth. Fold in peanut butter and mix well.

3. With wooden spoon, stir in oats, baking soda and butterscotch chips and mix well.

4. On baking sheet, drop dough with large spoon and flatten with fork.

5. Bake 8 to 10 minutes and cool.

Crackerjack Cookies

1 cup (2 sticks) butter, softened	250 ml
1 cup sugar	250 ml
1 cup packed brown sugar	250 ml
2 eggs	2
2 teaspoons vanilla	10 ml
2 cups flour	500 ml
1 teaspoon baking soda	5 ml
1 teaspoon baking powder	5 ml
2 cups quick-cooking oats	500 ml
2½ cups crispy rice cereal	625 ml
1 cup chopped pecans	250 ml

1. Preheat oven to 350° (176° C).

2. In mixing bowl, cream butter, both sugars, eggs and vanilla and beat well.

3. Stir in flour, baking soda and baking powder and mix well. Add remaining ingredients and mix well.

4. On lightly greased baking sheet, drop dough by teaspoonfuls and bake 8 to 10 minutes or until cookies brown slightly.

Special K Cookies

1 cup (2 sticks) butter, softened	250 ml
1 cup oil	250 ml
1 cup sugar	250 ml
1 cup packed light brown sugar	250 ml
1 egg	1
1 teaspoon vanilla	5 ml
1 cup Special K cereal	250 ml
1 cup flaked coconut	250 ml
1 cup quick-cooking oats	250 ml
3½ cups flour	875 ml
½ teaspoon salt	2 ml
1 teaspoon baking soda	5 ml
1 teaspoon cream of tartar	5 ml
1½ cups chopped pecans	375 ml

1. Preheat oven to 350° (176° C).

2. In large bowl, combine butter, oil, both sugars, egg, vanilla, cereal, coconut and oats and mix well.

3. In separate bowl, combine flour, salt, baking soda and cream of tartar.

4. Add dry ingredients to sugar-oats mixture and mix well. Fold in chopped pecans.

5. On greased baking sheet, drop dough by spoonfuls and bake 10 to 12 minutes. Cool.

Breakfast cereal was invented in 1863.

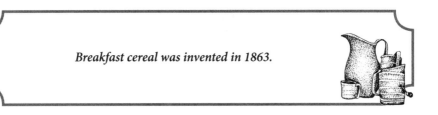

Classic Brown-Eyed Susans

1 cup butter, softened	250 ml
¼ cup sugar	60 ml
½ teaspoon almond extract	2 ml
2 cups flour	500 ml
½ teaspoon salt	2 ml
1 cup powdered sugar	250 ml
3 tablespoons cocoa	45 ml
1½ tablespoons hot water	22 ml
½ teaspoon vanilla	2 ml
Whole almonds	

1. Preheat oven to 350° (176° C). Beat butter and sugar until light and fluffy. Stir in almond extract.

2. Gradually add flour and salt and mix well after each addition. Form cookie dough into balls and place on cookie sheet. With bottom of glass or hand, flatten balls slightly.

3. Bake for 13 to 15 minutes or until light brown. Set aside to cool.

4. Mix powdered sugar and cocoa and gradually pour in hot water and vanilla. Mix well and frost cookies. Put whole almond on top of each cookie.

Gum-Drop Chews

1 cup flour	250 ml
½ teaspoon baking powder	2 ml
½ teaspoon baking soda	2 ml
⅛ teaspoon salt	.5 ml
1 egg	1
½ cup packed brown sugar	125 ml
½ cup sugar	125 ml
½ cup (1 stick) butter, softened	125 ml
1 teaspoon vanilla	5 ml
2 cups gum-drops, cut up	500 ml
1 cup oats	250 ml
1 cup chopped pecans	250 ml

1. Preheat oven to 350° (176° C).

2. In mixing bowl, combine flour, baking powder, baking soda and salt.

3. Add egg, both sugars, butter and vanilla and mix well. Gradually stir in dry ingredients.

4. Add gum-drops, oats and pecans and mix.

5. On baking sheet, drop dough by teaspoonfuls and bake 12 to 15 minutes.

For variation, use orange slices instead of gum drops.

Texas Ranger Cookies

1 cup shortening	250 ml
1¼ cups sugar	310 ml
1 cup packed brown sugar	250 ml
2 eggs	2
1 teaspoon vanilla	2 ml
2 cups flour	500 ml
1½ teaspoons baking soda	7 ml
1 teaspoon baking powder	5 ml
½ teaspoon salt	2 ml
2 cups quick-cooking oats	500 ml
2 cups crispy rice cereal	500 ml
1 (3½ ounce) can flaked coconut	1(100 g)
¾ cup chopped pecans	180 ml

1. Preheat oven to 350° (176° C).

2. In mixing bowl, cream shortening and both sugars. Add eggs and vanilla and mix until smooth.

3. In separate bowl, sift flour, soda, baking powder and salt. Add to creamed mixture and mix well.

4. Add remaining ingredients and mix. If mixture is too crumbly, add 1 teaspoon (5 ml) water.

5. On baking sheet, drop dough by tablespoonfuls and bake about 15 minutes or until cookies brown slightly. Makes about 5 dozen cookies.

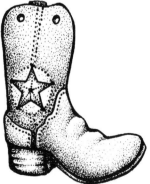

Coffee Cookies

4 large egg whites	4
3¾ cups sugar	930 ml
⅛ teaspoon salt	.5 ml
1 tablespoon instant coffee granules	15 ml
1¼ cups crushed corn flakes	310 ml
½ cup finely chopped pecans	125 ml

1. Preheat oven to 275° (135° C).

2. In mixing bowl, beat egg whites until stiff peaks form. Do not over beat.

3. In smaller bowl, combine sugar, salt and coffee granules. Gradually add sugar mixture to egg whites and beat again, but not vigorously.

4. Fold in corn flakes crumbs and pecans.

5. On greased baking sheet, drop dough by teaspoonfuls and bake 20 to 25 minutes.

6. Remove cookies from pan while still warm.

Ice Cream Cookies

⅓ cup butter	80 ml
1 pint (2 cups) vanilla ice cream, softened	500 ml
2 cups flour	500 ml
⅔ cup sugar	160 ml
1 teaspoon baking soda	5 ml
½ teaspoon salt	2 ml
1 teaspoon vanilla	5 ml
Sugar	

1. Preheat oven to 350° (176° C).

2. In large saucepan, melt butter over low heat. Remove from heat, stir in soft ice cream and blend well.

3. Mix in flour, sugar, baking soda, salt and vanilla and mix well until smooth.

4. On lightly greased baking sheets, drop dough by teaspoonfuls and sprinkle with granulated sugar.

5. Bake 10 to 12 minutes or until cookies turn light golden.

6. Remove from oven and immediately lift cookies from baking sheet to cool.

Classic Old-Fashioned Sour Cream Cookies

1½ to 2 cups sugar	375 to 500 ml
1 cup butter, softened	250 ml
2 eggs	2
1 cup sour cream	250 ml
1 teaspoon vanilla	5 ml
4 cups flour	1 L
1 teaspoon baking soda	5 ml
1 to 2 teaspoons baking powder	5 to 10 ml
½ teaspoon salt	2 ml

1. Cream sugar and butter until smooth. Add eggs, sour cream and vanilla and stir well.

2. In a separate bowl, combine flour, baking soda, baking powder and salt. Gradually add to sugar-butter mixture and beat after each addition. Chill overnight.

3. Sprinkle a little powdered sugar or flour on wax paper and roll dough out to about ¼-inch (.5 cm) thick. Cut into desired shapes and bake at 350° (176° C) just until brown.

Cream Cheese Cookies

¾ cup (1½ sticks) butter, softened	180 ml
1 (3 ounce) package cream cheese, softened	1(85 g)
1 egg yolk	1
1 (16 ounce) box powdered sugar	1(454 g)
1 teaspoon vanilla	5 ml
1 tablespoon lemon juice	15 ml
2 teaspoons grated lemon peel	10 ml
2 cups flour	500 ml
1 cup chopped pecans	250 ml
Extra powdered sugar	

1. Preheat oven to 300° (149° C).

2. In mixing bowl, cream butter, cream cheese and egg yolk and beat until light and fluffy.

3. Add sugar, vanilla, lemon juice and lemon peel and beat. Add flour and mix well. Stir in pecans.

4. On greased baking sheet, drop dough by teaspoonfuls and bake 20 to 25 minutes. (Cookies do not need to brown.)

5. While hot, dip tops of cookies in powdered sugar.

Potato Chip Crispies

¾ cup (1½ sticks) butter, softened	180 ml
¾ cup sugar	180 ml
1 egg yolk	1
1 teaspoon vanilla	5 ml
1½ cups flour	375 ml
¾ cup crushed potato chips	180 ml
½ cup chopped nuts	125 ml

1. Preheat oven to 350° (176° C).

2. In mixing bowl, cream butter, sugar, egg and vanilla. Add flour, chips and nuts and mix well.

3. On ungreased baking sheet, drop dough by teaspoonfuls and bake about 12 minutes or until cookies brown lightly.

These are really good and crunchy. You will never be able to eat just one.

A cookie sheet is a rectangle pan about 14 x 16 inches with no sides. A baking sheet is a rectangle pan about 10 x 15 inches with 1-inch sides. A 9 x 13-inch baking pan has sides 2 to 3 inches high.

Buffalo-Chip Cookies

1 cup (2 sticks) butter, softened	250 ml
1 cup shortening	250 ml
2 cups packed brown sugar	500 ml
2 cups sugar	500 ml
4 eggs	4
4 cups flour	1 L
2 teaspoons vanilla	10 ml
3¾ cups flour	930 ml
2 teaspoons baking soda	10 ml
2 teaspoons baking powder	10 ml
½ teaspoon salt	2 ml
2 cups corn flakes	500 ml
2 cups oats	500 ml
1 cup flaked coconut	250 ml
1 cup chopped pecans	250 ml
1 (6 ounce) package chocolate chips	1 (170 g)

1. Preheat oven to 325°(163° C).

2. In large mixing bowl, cream butter, shortening, both sugars, eggs and vanilla.

3. In separate bowl, add flour, baking soda, baking powder and salt and gradually add to sugar mixture. Stir in remaining ingredients and mix well.

4. Form cookies by using ¼ cup (60 ml) batter for each cookie (about 6 cookies on baking sheet).

5. Bake 15 minutes or until cookies brown lightly. Store in airtight container.

Whippersnappers

¾ cup packed brown sugar	180 ml
¾ cup sugar	180 ml
1½ cups shortening	375 ml
2 large eggs	2
1½ cups flour	375 ml
½ teaspoon baking soda	2 ml
½ teaspoon salt	2 ml
2¾ cups oats	680 ml
½ cup chopped pecans	125 ml
½ cup peanut butter	125 ml
1½ teaspoons vanilla	7 ml
1 (6 ounce) package chocolate chips	1(170 g)

1. Preheat over to 350° (176° C).

2. In mixing bowl, cream both sugars and shortening. Add eggs and beat.

3. In separate bowl, sift flour, baking soda and salt and add to sugar mixture.

4. Stir in oats, pecans, peanut butter, vanilla and chocolate chips.

5. On baking sheet, drop dough by teaspoonfuls and bake 12 to 14 minutes or until cookies begin to brown on edges.

Classic No-Bake Cookies

1 cup sugar	250 ml
1 cup milk	250 ml
5 tablespoons (½ stick) butter	75 ml
1 cup miniature marshmallows	250 ml
1 cup crushed graham crackers	250 ml

1. In saucepan, combine sugar, milk and butter. Bring to boil and cook 5 minutes.

2. Reduce heat, add marshmallows and cook and stir over low heat until marshmallows dissolve.

3. Stir in graham cracker crumbs and beat until mixture cools.

4. On wax paper, drop dough by spoonfuls or make into balls. Store in airtight container.

Kids' No-Bake

1 (14 ounce) can sweetened condensed milk	1 (420 g)
1 (12 ounce) package milk chocolate chips	1 (340 g)
3 cups vanilla wafer crumbs	750 ml
¾ cup chopped pecans	180 ml
1 teaspoon vanilla	5 ml

1. In large saucepan, combine condensed milk and chocolate chips.

2. Cook on low heat, stirring constantly, until chips melt. Stir in vanilla wafers, pecans and vanilla and roll into 1 to 2-inch (2.5 to 5 cm) balls.

3. Refrigerate until firm.

Wonder Bars

1¾ cups (3½ sticks) butter, divided	430 ml
2⅔ cups crushed graham crackers	660 ml
1½ cups crunchy peanut butter	375 ml
1 (16 ounce) package powdered sugar	1 (454 g)
2 (12 ounce) packages milk chocolate chips	2 (340 g)

1. In medium saucepan, melt 1½ cups (3 sticks) (375 ml) butter. Add crushed graham crackers, peanut butter and powdered sugar and mix well.

2. On greased baking sheet with sides, spread batter evenly with back of large spoon.

3. In saucepan, melt chocolate chips and remaining butter and quickly spread over graham cracker mixture.

4. Cool and cut in bars.

Nabisco graham crackers were developed in 1898.

Jazzy Graham Crackers

1 (14 ounce) box graham crackers	1 (420 g)
1 cup (2 sticks) butter, melted	250 ml
1 egg, beaten	1
½ cup milk	125 ml
1¼ cups sugar	310 ml
1 cup chocolate chips	250 ml
1 cup chopped pecans	250 ml
1 cup graham cracker crumbs	250 ml

Frosting:

½ cup (1 stick) butter, softened	125 ml
1 (16 ounce) box powdered sugar	1 (454 g)
About 2 tablespoons milk	30 ml
1 teaspoon vanilla	5 ml

1. Line greased 9 x 13-inch (23 x 33 cm) pan with whole graham crackers.

2. In saucepan over medium heat, combine butter, egg, milk and sugar and beat with spoon.

3. Heat mixture until it boils, then remove from heat and add chocolate chips, pecans and crumbs.

4. Slowly pour heated mixture over graham crackers in pan. Top with another layer of whole graham crackers. Chill.

5. In mixing bowl, combine all icing ingredients and beat until smooth. (If mixture is too stiff to spread, add 1 teaspoon (5 ml) milk until mixture reaches spreading consistency.)

6. Frost cookies and chill several hours before slicing in squares.

Snappy Oats

3 cups quick-rolled oats	750 ml
1 cup chocolate chips or white chocolate chips	250 ml
½ cup flaked coconut	125 ml
½ cup chopped pecans	125 ml
¾ cup candied cherries, optional	180 ml
2 cups sugar	500 ml
¾ cup (1½ sticks) butter	180 ml
½ cup evaporated milk	125 ml
¾ cup candied cherries, optional	180 ml

1. In large bowl, mix oats, chocolate chips, coconut, pecans and candied cherries.

2. In saucepan over high heat, bring sugar, butter and milk to rapid boil. Stir and boil 1½ minutes.

3. Pour hot mixture over oats, chocolate chips and coconut and stir until chocolate chips melt.

4. On wax paper, drop dough by teaspoonfuls.

5. Cool at room temperature and store in covered container.

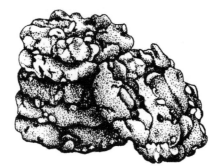

Quick Oatmeal Cookies

2¼ cups sugar	560 ml
½ cup chocolate chips	125 ml
½ cup milk	125 ml
½ cup (1 stick) butter	125 ml
1 teaspoon vanilla	5 ml
½ cup crunchy peanut butter	125 ml
2½ cups oats	625 ml

1. In saucepan, combine sugar, chocolate chips, milk and butter and bring to boil.

2. Remove from heat and add vanilla, peanut butter and oats. Stir well to blend all ingredients.

3. On wax paper, place heaping teaspoons batter.

4. Cool and store in airtight container.

*I*n 1908, Quaker Oats published its "Oat Cakes" cookie recipe on its packaging.

Classic Raggedy Anns

1⅓ cups graham cracker crumbs	330 ml
2 cups quick-cooking oats	500 ml
2 cups sugar	500 ml
2 tablespoons cocoa	30 ml
½ cup milk	125 ml
½ cup (1 stick) butter	125 ml
½ cup peanut butter	125 ml
1 teaspoon vanilla	5 ml

1. In bowl, combine graham cracker crumbs and oats and set aside.

2. In large saucepan, combine sugar, cocoa, milk and butter and heat to boiling. Boil 1 minute.

3. Remove from heat and stir in peanut butter and vanilla. Quickly add crumbs-oats mixture and blend.

4. On wax paper, drop dough by teaspoonfuls. Cool.

The Quaker Oats package was originally square. The familiar round package was introduced in 1915.

Coconut-Caramel Cookies

½ cup (1 stick) butter, softened	125 ml
½ cup whole milk	125 ml
1¼ cups sugar	310 ml
2 teaspoons vanilla	10 ml
¼ teaspoon salt	1 ml
28 caramels, unwrapped	28
3 cups oats	750 ml
1¼ cups flaked coconut	310 ml
⅓ cup slivered almonds, toasted	80 ml

1. In large heavy saucepan over medium heat, heat butter and milk until it boils.

2. Add sugar, vanilla and salt. Reduce heat and cook 1 minute.

3. Add caramels and stir about 4 minutes or just until caramels melt. Remove from heat and fold in oats, coconut and almonds.

4. On wax paper, drop dough by tablespoonfuls and let stand 1 hour or more before storing.

When using cookie cutters, chill the cut-out dough on the baking sheet before baking.

Krispy Date Cookies

1 cup sugar	250 ml
¼ cup (½ stick) butter	60 ml
2 eggs	2
1 (8 ounce) box pitted dates, cut up	1 (228 g)
3 cups crispy rice cereal	750 ml
1 cup flaked coconut	250 ml

1. In large saucepan, combine sugar, butter, eggs and dates. Bring to boil, reduce heat and cook and stir 5 minutes.

2. Add cereal and mix well. Rub shortening on hands and with heaping tablespoonfuls of dough, form into balls and roll in finely chopped pecans.

Scotch Crunchies

½ cup crunchy peanut butter	125 ml
1 (6 ounce) package butterscotch bits	1 (170 g)
2½ cups frosted flakes	560 ml
½ cup peanuts	125 ml

1. In large saucepan over low heat, stir and melt peanut butter and butterscotch bits.

2. When butterscotch bits melt, stir in cereal and peanuts.

3. On wax paper, drop dough by teaspoonfuls and chill until firm.

4. Store in airtight container.

Maraschino Cherubs

2 cups vanilla wafer crumbs	500 ml
¾ cup sugar	180 ml
⅓ cup sweetened condensed milk	80 ml
1 cup finely chopped pecans	250 ml
½ teaspoon cinnamon	2 ml
½ cup chopped maraschino cherries, well drained	125 ml
1 tablespoons lemon juice	15 ml

1. In mixing bowl, combine all ingredients and mix well.

2. Roll dough in small balls and place on wax paper until dough sets. Store in refrigerator.

Cocoa-Marshmallow Puffs

8 cups Cocoa Puff cereal	2 L
½ cut (1 stick) butter	125 ml
54 large marshmallows	54
1 (12 ounce) package milk chocolate chips	1 (340 g)
36 milk chocolate kisses	36

1. Place cereal in large bowl and set aside.

2. In heavy saucepan, combine butter and marshmallows. Cook on low heat, stirring constantly, until marshmallows melt.

3. Add chocolate chips and stir until chips melt. Pour over cereal and stir until well coated.

4. Spread evenly in buttered 10 x 15-inch (25 x 38 cm) pan and press down with back of wooden spoon.

5. Place kisses in middle of planned squares. Cool and cut into squares.

Chocolate-Marshmallow Squares

1 (12 ounce) package chocolate chips	1 (340 g)
1 cup butterscotch chips	250 ml
½ cup peanut butter	125 ml
1 (10 ounce) package miniature marshmallows	1 (248 g)
1 cup salted peanuts	250 ml

1. Grease 9 x 13-inch (23 x 33 cm) dish.

2. In large saucepan over low heat, combine chocolate chips, butterscotch chips and peanut butter and stir until chips melt.

3. Stir in marshmallows and peanuts and spread mixture in prepared dish. Cool and cut in squares.

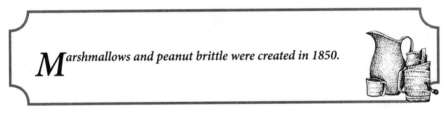

*M*arshmallows and peanut brittle were created in 1850.

Chocolate Drops

1 (6 ounce) package milk chocolate chips	1 (170 g)
⅔ cup chunky peanut butter	160 ml
4¼ cups cocoa-flavored crispy rice cereal	1 L + 60 ml

1. In double boiler, melt chocolate chips and stir in peanut butter. Gradually stir in cereal.

2. In 9 x 9-inch (23 x 23 cm) square dish, press mixture firmly.

3. Cut in bars to serve.

Krispies

1 cup white corn syrup	250 ml
1¼ cups sugar	310 ml
2 cups crunchy peanut butter	500 ml
4 cups crispy rice cereal	1 L

1. In saucepan, combine corn syrup and sugar and bring to rolling boil. Remove from heat, stir in peanut butter and cereal and mix well.

2. On wax paper, drop dough by teaspoonfuls and cool several minutes until treats are no longer sticky.

3. Store in airtight container.

Peanut Krispies

½ cup (1 stick) butter	125 ml
2 cups peanut butter	500 ml
1 (16 ounce) box powdered sugar	1 (454 g)
3½ cups crispy rice cereal	875 ml
¾ cup chopped peanuts	180 ml

1. In large saucepan, melt butter. Add peanut butter and powdered sugar and mix well.

2. Add cereal and peanuts and mix well.

3. On wax paper, drop dough by teaspoonfuls.

Classic Orange-Coconut Logs

3¼ cups vanilla wafer crumbs	810 ml
1 (16 ounce) box powdered sugar	1 (454 g)
2 cups chopped pecans	500 ml
1 (6 ounce) can frozen orange juice concentrate, thawed	1 (170 g)
½ cup (1 stick) butter, melted	125 ml
1 cup flaked coconut	250 ml

1. In mixing bowl, combine vanilla wafer crumbs, powdered sugar and pecans.

2. Stir in orange juice and butter and mix.

3. Shape dough in 2-inch (5 cm) fingers and roll in coconut. Refrigerate.

Classic Rocky Road Bars

1 (12 ounce) package semi-sweet chocolate morsels	1 (340 g)
1 (14 ounce) can sweetened condensed milk	1 (420 g)
2 tablespoons butter	30 ml
2 cups dry roasted peanuts	500 ml
1 (10 ounce) package miniature marshmallows	1 (284 g)

1. In top of double boiler, heat and stir chocolate morsels, milk and butter.

2. Remove from heat and stir in peanuts and marshmallows.

3. On wax paper-lined 9 x 13-inch (23 x 33 cm) pan, quickly spread mixture. Chill at least 2 hours.

4. Cut in bars and store in refrigerator.

Chocolate Sticks

1 (6 ounce) package chocolate chips	1 (170 g)
1 (6 ounce) package butterscotch chips	1 (170 g)
⅛ cup (¼ stick) butter	.5 ml
½ cup creamy peanut butter	125 ml
1 cup chopped pecans	250 ml
2 (1½ ounce) cans potato sticks	2 (40 g)

1. In double boiler or in microwave, melt chocolate chips, butterscotch chips, butter and peanut butter.

2. Stir in pecans and potato sticks.

3. On wax paper, drop mixture by rounded teaspoonfuls and chill just until firm.

Classic Haystacks

1 (12 ounce) package butterscotch morsels	1 (340 g)
2 cups chow mein noodles	500 ml
1 cup dry roasted peanuts	250 ml

1. In medium saucepan over low heat, melt butterscotch morsels.

2. Remove from heat, add noodles and peanuts and stir until each piece is coated.

3. On wax paper, drop haystacks from spoon and cool.

Frosted Pretzels

1 cup ready-to-spread vanilla frosting	250 ml
1 (10 ounce) bag large pretzel twists	1 (284 g)

1. In 2-cup (500 ml) glass measuring cup, spoon frosting and microwave on high 30 to 45 seconds (stir once) until frosting melts.

2. Dip half each pretzel into frosting and allow excess to drip.

3. Place on wax paper and let dry 2 hours.

White Chocolate Salties

8 (2 ounce) squares almond bark	8 (57 g)
6 ounces salted Spanish peanuts	170 g
3 cups thin pretzel sticks, broken up	750 ml

1. In large saucepan over low heat, stir and melt almond bark. Remove from heat.

2. Add peanuts and pretzels and stir until coated.

3. On wax paper, drop mixture by teaspoonfuls and chill 20 minutes or until firm.

Chocolate Crunchies

1 (20 ounce) package chocolate almond bark, broken	1 (570 g)
¾ cup light corn syrup	180 ml
⅛ cup (¼ stick) butter	.5 ml
2 teaspoons vanilla	10 ml
8 cups crispy rice cereal	2 L

1. In top of double boiler, combine chocolate, corn syrup and butter. Heat on low and cook, stir constantly until chocolate melts. Remove from heat and stir in vanilla.

2. In large mixing bowl, place cereal and pour chocolate mixture on top. Stir until cereal is well coated. In buttered 9 x 13-inch (23 x 33 cm) dish, quickly spoon mixture and press down firmly using back of spoon. Cool completely and cut in bars.

Jingle Bell Cookies

1 cup sugar	250 ml
½ cup (1 stick) butter	125 ml
½ cup evaporated milk	125 ml
1½ cups miniature marshmallows	375 ml
1½ cups graham cracker or vanilla wafer crumbs	375 ml
1 cup chopped pecans	250 ml

1. In saucepan, combine sugar, butter and evaporated milk. Boil 6 minutes, stirring constantly. Remove from heat, add marshmallows and stir until marshmallows melt. Stir in graham cracker crumbs and pecans.

2. With spoon, beat dough until it cools and thickens. Add eggs and flour and mix well. On buttered wax paper, quickly drop dough by tablespoonfuls. Store in covered container.

Pretzels to Love

1 cup sugar	250 ml
1¼ cups light corn syrup	310 ml
½ cup chunky peanut butter	125 ml
½ cup chopped peanuts	125 ml
2 cups broken pretzel sticks	500 ml
1 cup colored M&M candies	250 ml
5 cups crispy rice cereal	1 L + 250 ml

1. In microwave-safe bowl, combine sugar and corn syrup. Microwave on high 3 minutes or until sugar dissolves. Add peanut butter and mix well.

2. Stir in peanuts, pretzel sticks, M&M candies and rice cereal and stir until ingredients mix well.

3. In greased 10 x 15-inch (25 x 38 cm) baking dish, press mixture and let stand about 1 hour. Cut in bars to serve.

Orange Balls

1 (12 ounce) box vanilla wafers, crushed	1 (340 g)
½ cup (1 stick) butter, melted	125 ml
1 (16 ounce) package powdered sugar	1 (454 g)
1 (6 ounce) can frozen orange juice, thawed	1 (170 g)
1 cup finely chopped pecans	250 ml

1. In mixing bowl, combine wafers, butter, sugar and orange juice and mix well. Form into balls and roll in chopped pecans. Store in airtight container.

These work well in finger shapes too. They make
neat cookies for parties and teas.

Classic Bourbon Balls

3 cups crushed vanilla wafers	750 ml
1 cup very finely chopped pecans	250 ml
1⅔ cups sifted powdered sugar	410 ml
3 tablespoons light corn syrup	45 ml
1½ tablespoons cocoa	22 ml
⅓ cup bourbon	80 ml
1 teaspoon vanilla	5 ml
Powdered sugar	

1. In large mixing bowl, combine crushed vanilla wafers, pecans, powdered sugar, corn syrup, cocoa, bourbon and vanilla. Mix until ingredients blend well.

2. Roll in walnut-size balls and dust with sifted powdered sugar. Store in airtight container.

Classic Rum Balls

1 cup vanilla wafers, crushed	250 ml
1 cup powdered sugar	250 ml
1½ cups chopped pecans, divided	375 ml
2 tablespoons cocoa	30 ml
2 tablespoons light corn syrup	30 ml
¼ cup rum	60 ml
Powdered sugar	

1. Mix vanilla wafer crumbs, powdered sugar, 1 cup chopped pecans and cocoa. Stir in corn syrup and rum and mix well.

2. Shape in 1-inch balls and half in powdered sugar. Roll remaining balls in pecans. Makes about 3 dozen.

Coconut-Date Balls

1 (16 ounce) package sugar-rolled chopped dates	1 (454 g)
¼ cup (1 stick) butter	60 ml
2 egg yolks	2
¾ cup sugar	180 ml
1 teaspoon vanilla	5 ml
2 cups crispy rice cereal	500 ml
1¼ cups chopped pecans	310 ml
1 (4 ounce) can flaked coconut	1 (115 g)

1. In heavy skillet or saucepan over high heat, cook and stir dates, butter, egg yolks and sugar until mixture boils. Boil 5 minutes, stirring constantly.

2. Remove from heat and add vanilla, crispy rice cereal and pecans.

3. Shape dough in bite-size balls and roll in coconut.

These are a special treat during the holidays.

Shredded coconut was first introduced in 1895.

Grandma's Date-Fig Balls

*These are best if eaten within a day or two
or the cereal loses its crunchiness.*

½ cup (1 stick) butter	125 ml
1 cup sugar	250 ml
2 large eggs, lightly beaten	2
½ cup chopped dates	125 ml
½ cup chopped figs	125 ml
2½ cups crispy rice cereal	625 ml
⅓ cup chopped nuts	80 ml
⅓ cup shredded coconut	80 ml

1. Melt butter in large, heavy saucepan. Add sugar, eggs, dates and figs. Bring to boil over medium heat, stirring constantly with wooden spoon to prevent scorching.

2. Cook slowly until it thickens, about 6 minutes. Remove from heat and cool to lukewarm. Fold in cereal and nuts.

3. Form into small balls and roll in coconut. Cool on wax paper and store in airtight container. Yield: About 5 dozen cookies

Tip: Raisins may be substituted for figs.

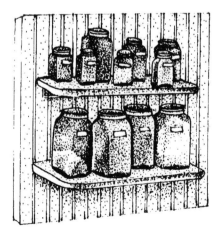

Pecan-Date Balls

½ cup (1 stick) butter	125 ml
1 cup sugar	250 ml
1 (8 ounce) box chopped dates	1 (228 g)
1 cup crispy rice cereal	250 ml
1 cup chopped pecans	250 ml
1 teaspoon vanilla	5 ml
Powdered sugar	

1. In large saucepan over medium heat, combine butter, sugar and chopped dates. Stir until all ingredients melt and blend well.

2. Remove from heat and add cereal, chopped pecans and vanilla. Stir to mix well.

3. Roll mixture in balls about ¾ inch (2 cm) in diameter. Drop balls, a few at a time, into small grocery sack or plastic bag with enough powdered sugar to cover.

4. Shake lightly until date balls are coated with sugar.

5. Store in airtight container.

Tip: These can also be frozen for later use.

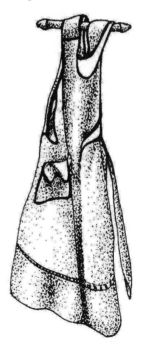

Nutty Butter Balls

1 cup (2 sticks) butter, softened	500 ml
⅔ cup sugar	160 ml
¼ teaspoon salt	1 ml
1 teaspoon almond extract	5 ml
1 teaspoon vanilla	5 ml
1 teaspoon butter flavoring	5 ml
2 cups flour	500 ml
1½ cups very finely chopped pecans	375 ml
Powdered sugar	

1. In mixing bowl, beat butter, sugar and salt and mix well. Add flavoring and mix well.

2. Chill several hours for easier handling. Shape dough in 1-inch (2.5 cm) balls and place on ungreased baking sheet.

3. Bake at 350° (176° C) for 10 to 12 minutes or until cookies brown slightly.

5. While cookies are warm, roll in powdered sugar.

Classic Ice Box Cookies

1 cup shortening	250 ml
¼ cup packed brown sugar	60 ml
1 cup sugar	250 ml
1 egg	1
¼ teaspoon salt	1 ml
1½ teaspoons vanilla	7 ml
2 cups flour	500 ml
2 teaspoons baking powder	10 ml
1 cup chopped pecans	250 ml

1. In mixing bowl, combine shortening, both sugars, egg, salt and vanilla and mix well.

2. Add flour and baking powder and mix well. Add pecans and mix.

3. Divide dough in half and roll each out in long jelly-roll shape on floured wax paper.

4. Roll up both jelly-roll shapes. Chill several hours.

5. When dough is thoroughly chilled, slice in ¼-inch (.5 cm) slices and place on baking sheet.

6. Bake at 350° (176° C) for 12 to 15 minutes or until cookies brown slightly.

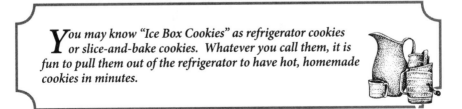

You may know "Ice Box Cookies" as refrigerator cookies or slice-and-bake cookies. Whatever you call them, it is fun to pull them out of the refrigerator to have hot, homemade cookies in minutes.

Chocolate Crinkles

¾ cup (1½ sticks) butter	180 ml
1½ cups cocoa	375 ml
2 cups sugar	500 ml
4 eggs	4
2 teaspoons vanilla	10 ml
2 cups flour	500 ml
2 teaspoons baking powder	10 ml
½ teaspoon salt	2 ml
1½ cups chopped pecans	375 ml
1 cup sifted powdered sugar	250 ml

1. In mixing bowl, combine butter, cocoa and sugar and mix well.

2. Add eggs one at a time and mix well. Stir in vanilla.

3. In separate bowl, combine flour, baking powder and salt and gradually stir into cocoa mixture. Fold in pecans. Chill dough several hours.

4. On wax paper, sprinkle powdered sugar. Shape into small balls and roll in powdered sugar.

5. On greased baking sheet, place balls 2 inches (5 cm) apart and bake at 350° (176° C) for about 10 minutes.

Pecan Slices

1 cup shortening	250 ml
1½ cups sugar	375 ml
1 egg, beaten	1
2 tablespoons orange juice	30 ml
1 tablespoon orange zest	15 ml
2¾ cups flour	680 ml
¼ teaspoon salt	1 ml
¼ teaspoon baking soda	1 ml
¾ cup very finely ground pecans	180 ml

1. In mixing bowl, cream shortening, sugar, egg, orange juice and orange zest.

2. In separate bowl, combine flour, salt, baking soda and pecans. Fold into shortening-sugar mixture and mix well.

3. Form dough in 3 long, thin rolls on wax paper. Chill several hours.

4. Slice rolls and place slices on greased baking sheet.

5. Bake at 350° (176° C) for 12 to 14 minutes.

6. Cool before storing.

*H*ave you ever "tip-toed" around your mother to get to the cookie dough in the refrigerator?

Cherry-Pecan Slices

2 cups powdered sugar	500 ml
1 cup (2 sticks) butter, softened	250 ml
1 egg	1
2 tablespoons milk	30 ml
1 teaspoon vanilla	5 ml
2¼ cups flour	560 ml
2 cups whole candied red cherries	500 ml
1 cup chopped pecans	250 ml
Extra flour	

1. In mixing bowl, cream sugar and butter until slightly fluffy. Add egg, milk and vanilla and mix.

2. Mix in flour (batter will be stiff). Stir in cherries and pecans and mix well. Chill dough 1 hour.

3. On wax paper, sprinkle small amount of flour. Shape dough in 2 (10 inch) (25 cm) rolls and wrap in wax paper. Chill at least 3 hours or overnight.

4. Cut dough rolls in ¼-inch (.5 cm) slices and place on ungreased baking sheets.

5. Bake at 350° (176° C) for 10 to 12 minutes or just until edges begin to brown.

6. Cool on wire racks and store in covered container.

The best way to keep refrigerated cookie dough from getting flat on one side when you slice it is to roll it on the counter after each slice. Another idea is to roll it one-quarter of the way around the roll after each slice.

Coconut-Cookie Slices

2 cups flour	500 ml
⅛ teaspoon salt	.5 ml
¼ teaspoon cinnamon	1 ml
1½ teaspoons baking powder	7 ml
½ cup (1 stick) butter, softened	125 ml
1½ cups sugar	375 ml
¼ cup packed brown sugar	60 ml
1 egg, beaten	1
1 teaspoon vanilla	5 ml
½ teaspoon lemon extract	2 ml
1 cup flaked coconut	250 ml

1. In mixing bowl, combine flour, salt, cinnamon and baking powder and set aside.

2. In mixing bowl, cream butter, sugar and brown sugar until fluffy. Add egg, vanilla and lemon extract and mix well.

3. Fold in coconut and dry ingredients and blend well.

4. Shape dough in 2-inch (5 cm) rolls and wrap in wax paper. Cover and chill several hours or overnight.

5. When ready to bake, slice cookies in ¼-inch (.5 cm) slices and place on greased baking sheet.

6. Bake at 350° (176° C) for 8 to 10 minutes or until cookies turn golden brown.

Cookies Dressed for Santa

1 cup (2 sticks) butter, softened	250 ml
1½ cups sugar	375 ml
1 egg, beaten	1
1 teaspoon vanilla	5 ml
2¾ cups flour	680 ml
1 teaspoon baking powder	5 ml
¼ teaspoon salt	1 ml
1 (16 ounce) jar maraschino cherries, drained, finely chopped	1(454 g)
1 cup slivered almonds	250 ml
⅓ cup red decorator sugar crystals	80 ml

1. In mixing bowl, beat butter and sugar until creamy. Gradually add egg and vanilla and mix well.

2. Add flour, baking powder and salt to creamy mixture and beat well.

3. Drain chopped cherries on several paper towels to remove all moisture. Stir cherries and almonds into dough. Cover and chill several hours.

4. Shape dough in 2 (8½ inch) (21 cm) long rolls. Roll dough in decorator sugar crystals. Wrap rolls in wax paper and chill until firm (or freeze).

5. Preheat oven to 350° (176° C).

6. With sharp knife, slice rolls in 1-inch (2.5 cm) slices. On greased baking sheet, place slices and bake 8 to 10 minutes. Cool before storing.

Use different decorations and sprinkles for different holidays.

Traditional Sand Tarts

2 cups powdered sugar	500 ml
1 cup (2 sticks) butter, softened	250 ml
1 teaspoon vanilla extract	5 ml
3 large eggs, lightly beaten	3
4 cups flour, sifted	1 L
1 large egg, well beaten	1
½ cup sugar	125 ml
1½ teaspoons ground cinnamon	7 ml
½ cup finely chopped pecans	125 ml
Powdered sugar	

1. Preheat oven to 350° (176° C). Cream sugar and butter in large mixing bowl and mix vigorously until smooth, light and creamy.

2. Stir in vanilla and eggs slowly until they blend well. Stir in flour and blend thoroughly. Chill, covered, for several hours.

3. Keep dough cold and roll small amount of dough at a time. Roll very thin, ⅛ inch (.5 cm) thick using very little flour on board. Form into crescents and place on greased cookie sheet. Brush with bit of beaten egg and top with sugar, cinnamon and nuts.

4. Bake on middle rack until golden brown, about 7 minutes. Grease cookie sheet each time after removing baked cookies.

5. Remove and cool on clean linen towels. Roll in powdered sugar. These cookies taste better after being stored in airtight containers for a day or two. Yield: About 9 to 10 dozen 2-inch (5 cm) cookies.

Classic Rolled Cookie Cut-Outs

½ cup butter, softened	125 ml
1 cup sugar	250 ml
1 egg	1
1 tablespoon cream	15 ml
½ teaspoon vanilla	2 ml
2 cups flour	500 ml
¼ teaspoon salt	1 ml
1 teaspoon baking powder	5 ml

1. Cream butter and slowly add sugar. Beat until light and fluffy. Combine egg, cream and vanilla, add to butter mixture and beat to mix.

2. In separate bowl, combine flour, baking powder and salt. Add a little flour mixture to butter mixture and mix after each addition.

3. Refrigerate for at least 3 to 4 hours.

4. Preheat oven to 375° (176° C). Sprinkle flour over wax paper and roll dough to ¼-inch (.5 cm) thickness. Use favorite cookie cutters to make shapes. Use spatula to move cookies from wax paper to cookie sheet. Repeat process with leftover dough.

5. Bake for about 5 to 8 minutes. Makes about 5 dozen.

Classic Old-Fashioned Tea Cakes

3¼ cups flour	810 ml
1 teaspoon baking soda	5 ml
½ teaspoon salt	2 ml
½ cup (1 stick) butter, softened	125 ml
1 cup sugar	250 ml
1 egg, beaten	1
1½ teaspoons vanilla	7 ml
½ cup sour cream	125 ml

1. Preheat oven to 350° (176° C).

2. In mixing bowl, sift flour, baking soda and salt.

3. In separate bowl, combine butter, sugar, egg and vanilla and beat on medium speed 2 minutes.

4. Add sour cream gradually to flour mixture and beat on low speed.

5. On lightly-floured surface, roll dough to ¼-inch (.5 cm) thickness. Cut cookies with floured cookie cutter and place on greased baking sheet.

6. Bake 10 to 12 minutes. (Watch closely because cookies do not need to brown.)

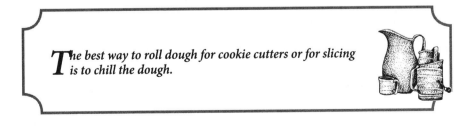

The best way to roll dough for cookie cutters or for slicing is to chill the dough.

Classic Biscochitos Cut-Outs

3 cups flour	750 ml
1½ teaspoons anise seed	7 ml
1½ teaspoons baking powder	7 ml
½ teaspoon salt	2 ml
1 cup shortening	250 ml
½ teaspoon vanilla	2 ml
1½ cups sugar	375 ml
2 eggs	2
¼ cup orange juice	60 ml
2 teaspoons cinnamon	10 ml
½ cup sugar	125 ml

1. Preheat oven to 350°(176° C).

2. In large bowl, combine flour, anise seed, baking powder and salt and set aside.

3. In mixing bowl with electric mixer, beat shortening and vanilla until creamy. Add sugar and beat until fluffy. Blend in eggs and beat again. Alternately add flour mixture and orange juice and mix well after each addition.

4. On lightly floured board, divide dough in half and roll out 1 portion at a time to ¼-inch (.5 cm) thickness.

5. With fancy cookie cutters, cut out cookies. As you cut cookies, add scraps to remaining dough. (If dough becomes too sticky to handle, chill briefly.)

6. In small bowl, mix cinnamon and sugar and sprinkle over cookies.

7. Bake 8 to 10 minutes or until edges just begin to brown. Cool.

Christmas Cut-Outs

6 tablespoons (¾ stick) butter, softened	90 ml
1 cup sugar	250 ml
2 eggs	2
1 teaspoon vanilla	5 ml
2½ cups flour	625 ml
1 teaspoon baking powder	5 ml
1 teaspoon salt	5 ml
Powdered sugar	

1. In large mixing bowl, combine butter, sugar, eggs and vanilla and beat until ingredients blend well and are light and fluffy.

2. In separate bowl, combine flour, baking powder and salt and add gradually to sugar mixture. Beat well.

3. Cover dough and chill in refrigerator 1 hour.

4. Sprinkle powdered sugar on countertop. Roll dough ⅛-inch (.25 cm) thick and cut in desired shapes.

5. Bake at 350° (176° C) for 6 to 8 minutes.

6. Remove cookies immediately from baking sheet and cool before decorating.

A mixture of powdered sugar and flour should be sprinkled on the counter before rolling out cookie dough. The powdered sugar keeps the dough from sticking and getting tough.

Classic Old-Timey Gingerbread Cookies

1 cup lard or (2 sticks) butter, softened	250 ml
1 cup sorghum or molasses	250 ml
1 cup packed brown sugar	250 ml
½ cup hot water	125 ml
2 eggs	2
6 cups flour	1.5 L
2 teaspoons ginger	10 ml
2 teaspoons cinnamon	10 ml
1 teaspoon baking soda	5 ml
½ teaspoon salt	2 ml

1. Combine butter, molasses, brown sugar and hot water and mix well. Stir in eggs and mix well.

2. In separate bowl, combine flour, ginger, cinnamon, baking soda and salt. Gradually pour flour mixture into butter mixture a little at a time and beat after each addition. Cover dough and chill overnight.

3. Preheat oven to 350° (176° C). On non-stick surface roll out dough to about ¼ to ½ inch (.5 cm) thickness and cut out gingerbread men with cookie cutters. (Use your favorite shapes if you don't have men or cut them out free hand and make your own creative shapes.)

4. Bake for about 10 minutes or until top springs back. These freeze well.

Though the practice of baking gingerbread is centuries old, modern gingerbread may owe its popularity to the 19-century publication of the German fairy tale, Hansel and Gretel. Countries throughout Europe still bake traditional gingerbread houses, cakes and cookies. The popularity of gingerbread in America is especially evident at Christmastime, when children and adults alike participate in elaborate contests to see who can design the most breathtaking creation.

Buttery Lemon Cookies

1 pound (4 sticks) butter, softened	454 g
2 cups sugar	500 ml
2 eggs, beaten	2
4 cups flour	1 L
½ teaspoon baking powder	2 ml
1 teaspoon salt	5 ml
1 tablespoon lemon extract	15 ml

1. Preheat oven to 350° (176° C).

2. In mixing bowl, cream butter and sugar until light and fluffy. Add eggs and beat again.

3. In separate bowl, combine flour, baking powder and salt. Add dry ingredients to butter-sugar mixture. Stir in lemon extract.

4. Place batter in cookie press and press to desired shape on baking sheet.

5. Bake 9 to 11 minutes or until edges brown lightly. Cool before storing.

There is no substitute for butter in baking. Margarine, light and whipped butter contain water and do not contain enough fat for baking.

Holiday Spritz Cookies

½ cup plus 2 tablespoons (1¼ sticks) butter, softened	280 ml
1¼ cups sugar	310 ml
1 egg, well beaten	1
1 teaspoon almond flavoring	5 ml
Food coloring, optional	
3 cups flour	750 ml
1 teaspoon baking powder	5 ml

1. In mixing bowl with electric mixer, cream butter and sugar.

2. Add egg and almond flavoring and beat well. To add a holiday touch, add food coloring of your choice.

3. Stir flour and baking powder into creamed mixture.

4. Fill cookie press with dough, press dough in desired shapes on ungreased baking sheet.

5. Bake at 350° (176° C) for about 8 minutes or until cookies brown lightly.

*Use some of the decorative icings or sprinkles
found in grocery store to decorate cookies.*

Frostings For Cookies

Butter-Cream Frosting:

4 tablespoons (½ stick) butter, softened	60 ml
2 tablespoons hot milk	30 ml
½ teaspoon vanilla	2 ml
1¼ cups sifted powdered sugar	310 ml

1. Stir butter vigorously until soft and creamy. Add hot milk, vanilla and a little powdered sugar, mix and gradually stir in remaining powdered sugar until frosting is spreading consistency. Add food coloring if desired. Use on any baked cookie. It's great!

Chocolate Frosting:

1 (1 ounce) square unsweetened chocolate or 3 tablespoons cocoa	45 ml
2 tablespoons butter, melted	30 ml
¼ cup evaporated milk or cream	60 ml
¼ teaspoon salt	1 ml
1 teaspoon vanilla	5 ml
1½ to 2 cups sifted powdered sugar	375 to 500 ml

1. In saucepan melt chocolate and butter and set aside to cool. When cool, add evaporated milk, salt and vanilla and gradually stir in powdered sugar until frosting is spreading consistency. This is great on peanut butter cookies, brownies, oatmeal cookies, shortbread or sugar cookies.

Cream Cheese Frosting:

1 (3 ounce) package cream cheese, softened	1 (85 g)
2 tablespoons milk	30 ml
1½ cups sifted powdered sugar	375 ml
¼ teaspoon salt	1 ml
½ teaspoon vanilla	2 ml

1. Beat cream cheese until fluffy. Add milk, powdered sugar, salt and vanilla and blend well. Spread on brownies, all kinds of bars and chocolate, date, fruit or drop cookies.

More Frostings For Cookies

Coconut Frosting:

¼ cup boiling water	60 ml
1 cup miniature marshmallows	250 ml
2 tablespoons butter	30 ml
1 cup shredded coconut	250 ml

1. In small saucepan combine boiling water, marshmallows and butter and stir until marshmallows melt. Remove from heat and stir in coconut. This is terrific on brownies, bars, chocolate, sugar and peanut butter cookies.

Lemon Frosting:

2 tablespoons butter, softened	30 ml
1½ cups sifted powdered sugar	375 ml
1 lemon	1
¼ teaspoon salt	60 ml

1. Blend butter and powdered sugar until creamy. Add juice and grated rind of lemon with salt and mix. Spread on cooled cookies such as molasses, orange, pineapple and sugar.

Peanut Butter Frosting:

¼ cup peanut butter	60 ml
2 tablespoons butter, melted	30 ml
½ cup packed brown sugar	125 ml
2 tablespoons hot coffee	30 ml
1½ cups sifted powdered sugar	375 ml
½ teaspoon vanilla	2 ml

1. Combine peanut butter, butter, brown sugar and hot coffee in saucepan and stir over low heat until sugar dissolves. Remove from heat and cool slightly before adding powdered sugar. Stir powdered sugar and vanilla to mix well. Great on brownies, oatmeal cookies, gum-drop cookies and sugar cookies.

Classic Monkey Faces

½ cup butter, softened	125 ml
1 cup sugar	250 ml
1 egg	1
1 tablespoon cream	15 ml
½ teaspoon vanilla	2 ml
1½ cups flour	375 ml
¼ teaspoon salt	1 ml
1 teaspoon baking powder	5 ml
Raisins	

1. Preheat oven to 375° (190° C). Cream butter and slowly add sugar. Beat until light and fluffy. Combine egg, cream and vanilla, add to butter mixture and beat to mix.

2. In a separate bowl, combine flour, baking powder and salt. Add a little flour mixture to butter mixture and mix after each addition.

4. Roll into 2-inch (5 cm) balls and place onto greased cookie sheet. Mash each ball about half way down. Use 2 raisins to make eyes and 3 raisins to make a mouth. (You get some pretty funny looking faces when they cook.)

5. Bake for about 8 to 10 minutes. Makes about 5 dozen.

Tip: If you don't like raisins, see what else you can come up with for eyes and mouths.

When using cookie cutters, especially plastic cookie cutters, dip the cookie cutters in warm vegetable oil so the edges will cut cleanly.

Classic Sand Tarts

1 cup (2 sticks) butter, softened	250 ml
1 cup powdered sugar	250 ml
2 cups sifted flour	500 ml
1 cup chopped pecans	250 ml
1 teaspoon vanilla	5 ml
Powdered sugar	

1. Preheat oven to 325° (163° C). In mixing bowl, cream butter and sugar. Add flour, pecans and vanilla and mix.

2. Shape dough into crescents and place on ungreased baking sheet. Bake 20 minutes. Cool and roll tarts in extra powdered sugar.

Praline Grahams

⅓ (16 ounce) package graham crackers	152 g
¾ cup (1½ sticks) butter	180 ml
½ cup sugar	125 ml
1 cup chopped pecans	250 ml

1. Preheat oven to 300° (149° C). Separate each graham cracker into 4 sections. Arrange in jelly-roll pan with edges touching.

2. In saucepan, melt butter and stir in sugar and pecans. Bring to boil and cook and stir 3 minutes. Spread mixture evenly over graham crackers.

3. Bake 10 to 12 minutes. Remove from pan and cool on wax paper. Break in smaller pieces to serve.

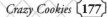

Double-Dutch Pizza Cookie

¾ cup (1½ sticks) butter, softened	180 ml
1 cup sugar	250 ml
1 egg	1
1 teaspoon vanilla	5 ml
1½ cups flour	375 ml
¼ cup cocoa	60 ml
½ teaspoon baking soda	2 ml
¼ teaspoon salt	1 ml
¾ cup plain M&M candies, divided	180 ml
¾ cup chopped pecans, divided	180 ml
1 cup miniature marshmallows	250 ml
¼ cup flaked coconut	60 ml

1. Preheat oven to 350°(176° C).

2. In mixing bowl, cream butter and sugar until light and fluffy. Beat in egg and vanilla.

3. In separate bowl, combine flour, cocoa, baking soda and salt. Gradually add to sugar mixture and mix well.

4. Fold in ¼ cup (60 ml) M&M candies and ¼ cup (60 ml) pecans.

5. Lightly grease 12-inch (30 cm) round pizza pan and line with parchment paper. Spread dough on pan to within one-half inch of edge. Sprinkle with remaining candy and pecans. Sprinkle marshmallows evenly over dough.

6. Bake 15 to 18 minutes or until edges set. Do not overbake. As soon as cookie is out of oven, sprinkle with coconut.

7. Cool in pan 15 minutes. Gently remove cookie with liner to wire rack to finish cooling. Cut in wedges.

Fill-A-Tart

Tart Shell:

6 tablespoons butter, softened	90 ml
1 (3 ounce) package cream cheese, softened	1 (85 g)
1 cup flour	250 ml

Filling:

2 tablespoons butter, softened	30 ml
½ cup sugar	125 ml
½ cup packed light brown sugar	125 ml
1 egg, beaten	1
⅔ cup finely chopped pecans	160 ml
1 teaspoon vanilla	5 ml

1. In mixing bowl, cream butter and cream cheese. Fold in flour and blend well.

2. Form into 1 large ball of dough. Divide dough in 24 equal balls.

3. In palm, flatten each ball into a circle and press circles into miniature muffin pan to form tart shells.

4. Preheat oven to 350° (176° C) while you make filling.

5. In mixing bowl, cream butter, both sugars and egg and mix well. Add pecans and vanilla.

6. Spoon filling into each shell. Bake about 20 minutes.

7. Cool before removing tarts from muffin pan.

Pecan Cups

Shell:

1 cup (2 sticks) butter	250 ml
1 (8 ounce) package cream cheese, softened	1 (228 g)
Dash salt	
2 cups flour	500 ml

Filling:

2 eggs, lightly beaten	2
¼ cup sugar	60 ml
1¼ cups packed brown sugar	310 ml
3 tablespoons butter, melted	45 ml
1¼ cups chopped pecans	310 ml
½ teaspoon vanilla	2 ml

1. Preheat oven to 350° (176° C).

2. In mixing bowl, whip butter and cream cheese until fluffy. Add salt and flour and mix well. Refrigerate dough until firm enough to handle.

3. After chilling, form chilled dough in small balls. In lightly buttered miniature 24-muffin pan, press dough to form cups.

4. In mixing bowl, combine eggs, sugar, brown sugar, butter, chopped pecans and vanilla and mix well. Pour mixture in shells.

5. Bake at 350° (176° C) for 30 minutes.

Chunky Chocolate Cookies

Truly this is the cookie for a chocoholic. These soft chocolate cookies are studded with dark chocolate and white chocolate chips.

Ingredients for jar:

⅔ cup packed dark brown sugar	160 ml
½ cup sugar	125 ml
1½ cups flour	375 ml
⅓ cup cocoa powder	80 ml
½ teaspoon baking soda	2 ml
Pinch salt	
¾ cup semi-sweet chocolate chips	375 ml
¾ cup white chocolate chips	375 ml

Instructions for jar:

1. In 1-quart (1 L) jar, pack brown sugar in bottom and make as level as possible. Pour sugar over top and level.

2. In small bowl, combine flour, cocoa powder, baking soda and salt. Mix well. Gently spoon flour mixture over sugar. Level carefully, then tamp down.

3. Pour semi-sweet chocolate chips and sprinkle white chocolate on top over flour and level. Place lid on jar and attach with gift tag and directions for baking.

(Continued on next page.)

(Continued)

Instructions for baking:

1 egg	**1**
¾ cup (1½ sticks) butter, softened	**180 ml**

1. Preheat oven to 350° (176° C). Pour contents of jar into large mixing bowl. Add 1 egg and ¾ cup (1½ sticks) (180 ml) softened butter. Beat on low speed or by hand until mixture blends thoroughly.

2. Drop by heaping teaspoonfuls onto ungreased cookie sheet. Bake for 13 to 15 minutes. Remove from oven and cool cookies on cookie sheet for 1 minute. Transfer to cooling rack. Makes about 3 dozen.

Spicy Oatmeal-Raisin Cookies

Delicious, soft, oatmeal-raisin cookies have a light spicy flavor. As they bake, their aroma fills the kitchen with a sweet, homey fragrance.

Ingredients for jar:

¾ cup packed light brown sugar	180 ml
⅓ cup sugar	80 ml
¾ teaspoon allspice	4 ml
¾ teaspoon baking powder	4 ml
⅛ teaspoon baking soda	.5 ml
1 cup flour	250 ml
1 cup quick-cooking oats	250 ml
¾ cup raisins	180 ml
½ cup chopped walnuts	125 ml

Instructions for jar:

1. In 1-quart (1 L) jar, pack brown sugar in bottom and make as level as possible. Pour sugar over top and level.

2. In small bowl, combine allspice, baking powder, baking soda and flour. Mix well. Gently spoon flour mixture over sugar. Level carefully, then tamp down.

3. Pour oats over flour and level. Sprinkle raisins on top and press down. Sprinkle nuts over raisins. Place lid on jar and attach with gift tag and directions for baking.

(Continued on next page.)

(Continued)

Instructions for baking:

1 egg	**1**
½ cup (1 stick) butter, softened	**125 ml**

1. Preheat oven to 375° (190° C). Pour mixture in jar into large mixing bowl. Add 1 egg and ½ cup (1 stick) (125 ml) butter.

2. Beat on low speed or mix by hand until mixture blends thoroughly.

3. Drop by rounded teaspoonfuls onto ungreased cookie sheet. Bake for 10 to 12 minutes.

4. Remove from oven and cool cookies on sheet for 1 minute. Transfer to cooling rack. Makes 2 to 2 ½ dozen.

Icing, optional:

1 cup powdered sugar, divided	**250 ml**
1 to 2 tablespoons milk	**15 to 30 ml**
¼ teaspoon vanilla	**1 ml**

1. In small bowl, combine powdered sugar with 1 tablespoon (15 ml) milk and vanilla. Stir until smooth, adding additional milk as necessary until drizzling consistency is reached. Drizzle over cookies and let set.

Hearty Trail Mix Cookies

These hearty cookies are filled with natural goodness--oats, raisins and coconut--as well as with a chocolate treat. They're not only delicious, but colorful too. The candies provide a rainbow of color.

Ingredients for jar:

½ cup packed brown sugar	125 ml
¼ cup sugar	60 ml
1 cup quick-cooking oats	250 ml
1 cup flour	250 ml
½ teaspoon baking powder	2 ml
⅛ teaspoon baking soda	.5 ml
½ cup raisins	125 ml
½ cup coconut	125 ml
½ cup M&M candies	125 ml

Instructions for jar:

1. In 1-quart (1 L) jar, pack brown sugar in bottom and make as level as possible. Pour sugar over top and level. Pour oats over sugar and level.

2. In small bowl, combine flour, baking powder and baking soda. Mix well. Gently spoon flour mixture over oats. Level carefully, then tamp down.

3. Sprinkle raisins over flour mixture, level and smooth edges to make them even. Sprinkle raisins on top and press down. Sprinkle coconut over raisins and press down.

4. Sprinkle candies on top. Press down, place lid on jar and attach with gift tag and directions for baking.

(Continued on next page.)

(Continued)

Instructions for baking:

1 egg	**1**
6 tablespoons butter, softened	**90 ml**

1. Preheat oven to 375° (190° C). Empty contents of jar into large mixing bowl. Add 1 egg and 6 tablespoons (90 ml) softened butter.

2. Beat on low speed or by hand to blend, then drop by heaping teaspoonfuls onto ungreased cookie sheet. Bake for 10 to 12 minutes or until edges are light brown.

3. Remove from oven and cool cookies on cookie sheet for 1 minute, then transfer to cooling rack. Makes about 3 dozen.

Peanutty Clusters

Crispy cookies burst with peanut flavor and are enhanced by butterscotch candies.

Ingredients for jar:

½ cup packed light brown sugar	125 ml
½ cup sugar	125 ml
¾ cup cocktail peanuts	180 ml
1½ cups flour	375 ml
¾ teaspoon baking soda	180 ml
½ teaspoon baking powder	125 ml
1/4 teaspoon salt	1 ml
1 cup butterscotch-flavored baking chips	250 ml
½ cup shredded coconut	125 ml

Instructions for jar:

1. Place brown sugar in 1-quart (1 L) jar and press down evenly. Pour sugar evenly over brown sugar. Sprinkle peanuts over sugar press down.

2. In medium bowl, combine flour, baking soda, baking powder and salt. Mix well. Pour half of mixture over peanuts and press down firmly.

3. Pour butterscotch chips over flour in jar and top with remaining flour. Place coconut on top of flour and press down firmly. Place lid on jar and attach with gift tag and directions for baking.

(Continued on next page.)

(*Continued*)

Instructions for baking:

½ cup (1 stick) butter, softened	125 ml
½ cup creamy peanut butter	125 ml
1 egg	1

1. Preheat oven to 375° (190° C). Empty contents of jar into large bowl and add butter, creamy peanut butter and egg.

2. Beat on low speed or by hand to blend. Roll heaping teaspoonfuls of dough into balls and place 3 inches (7.6 cm) apart on ungreased cookie sheet. Flatten with bottom of glass dipped in sugar.

3. Bake for 10 to 12 minutes or until edges are brown. Remove from oven and cool cookies on cookie sheet for 1 minute before transferring to cooling rack. Makes about 4 dozen.

Wholesome Peanut Butter Cookies

These soft peanut butter cookies are a hit.
The oats add a wonderful texture.

Ingredients for jar:

½ cup packed brown sugar	125 ml
1 cup sugar	250 ml
2 cups quick-cooking oats	500 ml
1 cup plus	250 ml +
2 tablespoons flour	30 ml
1 teaspoon baking powder	5 ml
½ teaspoon baking soda	2 ml
1/4 teaspoon salt	1 ml

Instructions for jar:

1. Place brown sugar in 1-quart jar and press down evenly. Pour sugar over brown sugar and smooth top. Pour oats over sugar.

2. In small bowl, mix flour, baking powder, baking soda and salt. Pour half of mixture on oats and press down firmly.

3. Add remaining flour mixture a little at a time, pressing down after each addition. (It will be a tight squeeze.) Place lid on jar and attach with gift tag and directions for baking.

(Continued on next page.)

(Continued)

Instructions for baking:

2 eggs	**2**
½ cup crunchy or creamy peanut butter	**125 ml**
¾ cup (1½ sticks) butter, softened	**375 ml**
1½ cups chocolate chips, optional	**375 ml**

1. Preheat oven to 375° (190° C). Empty contents of jar into large bowl. Add eggs, peanut butter and butter. If desired, stir in chocolate chips. Beat on low speed to blend.

2. Drop by heaping teaspoonfuls onto ungreased cookie sheet. Bake for 10 to 12 minutes or until edges are light brown.

3. Remove from oven and cool cookies on cookie sheet for 1 minute before transferring to cooling rack. Makes 4 to 4½ dozen.

Holiday Honey-Spice Cookies

These golden-colored crispy cookies that are sweet and full of citrus and spice flavor. They make a lovely gift at the holidays.

Ingredients for jar:

1 cup sugar	250 ml
1 cup packed light brown sugar	250 ml
2½ cups flour	625 ml
1 teaspoon cinnamon	5 ml
½ teaspoon ground cloves	2 ml
⅛ teaspoon ground nutmeg	.5 ml
1 tablespoon dried, ground lemon peel*	15 ml
1 tablespoon dried, ground orange peel*	15 ml
1 teaspoon baking soda	5 ml

Instructions for jar:

1. Pour sugar evenly in 1-quart (1 L) jar. Place brown sugar on top and pack down evenly.

2. In medium bowl, combine flour with remaining ingredients and mix well. Spoon flour mixture over brown sugar in jar and press down firmly after each addition. Place lid on jar to close and attach with gift tag and directions for baking.

(Continued on next page.)

*Dried, ground lemon peel and orange peel are found in the spice section of the grocery store.

(*Continued*)

Instructions for baking:

½ cup honey	125 ml
1/4 cup (½ stick) butter, softened	60 ml
1 egg	1
2 tablespoons milk	30 ml

1. Preheat oven to 350° (176° C). Empty contents of jar into large mixing bowl. Add honey, butter, egg and milk.

2. Beat on low speed or by hand until dough mixes completely. Roll pieces of dough into 1-inch (2.5 cm) balls and place 3 inches (7.6 cm) apart on lightly greased cookie sheet.

3. Bake for 10 to 12 minutes or until cookies are golden brown. Remove from oven and cool cookies on cookie sheet for 1 minute, then transfer to cooling rack. Makes 3½ to 4 dozen.

Orange-Sugar Cookies

These delicately-flavored sugar cookies have a hint of orange and the distinct flavor of almonds. They look so pretty in the jar with the alternating bands of orange. To make this an extra-special gift, attach a pretty cookie cutter to the jar with a ribbon.

Ingredients for jar:

1 cup sugar	250 ml
4 drops red food coloring	4
4 drops yellow food coloring	4
3 cups flour	750 ml
3 tablespoons dried, ground orange peel*	45 ml
1 teaspoon baking soda	5 ml
2 teaspoons baking powder	10 ml
½ cup finely ground almonds, toasted**	125 ml

Instructions for jar:

1. Place sugar in small bowl. Add red and yellow food coloring and stir well until sugar is evenly colored. (You'll end up with a nice orange color.) Allow to dry several minutes.

2. In medium bowl, combine flour, orange peel, baking soda and baking powder. Stir well to mix. Place half sugar in 1-quart (1 L) jar and smooth. Spoon half flour mixture on top and press down, smoothing out top.

3. Place remaining half of sugar over flour layer and press down evenly. Spoon remaining half of flour on top, press down and smooth over.

4. Place toasted almond on top of flour and press down firmly. (It will be a tight squeeze.) Place lid on jar and attach with gift tag and directions for baking.

(Continued on next page.)

(Continued)

Instructions for baking:

½ cup (1 stick) butter, softened	125 ml
½ teaspoon vanilla extract	2 ml
1 egg	1
½ cup milk	125 ml

1. Place contents of jar into large bowl. Add butter, vanilla, egg and milk. Beat on low speed to blend.

2. For drop cookies, drop dough by rounded teaspoonful onto ungreased cookie sheet. For rolled cookies, refrigerate dough for a couple of hours to chill to make it easier to work with.

3. Roll out on lightly floured surface to 1/4 inch thick. Cut with cookie cutter and place cut-outs on ungreased cookie sheet.

4. Bake at 350° (176° C) for 10 minutes. Remove cookies from oven and cool on cookie sheet for 1 minute, then transfer to cooling rack. Makes 3½ to 4 dozen.

Dried, ground orange peel is found in the spice section of your grocery store.

**To toast the almonds and bring out their flavor, place ground nuts on cookie sheet and bake at 350° (176° C) for about 5 minutes until they are light brown. Be sure to check them frequently because they can burn quickly. Cool completely before adding to jar.*

Chocolate Snickerdoodles

This is a spin on an old favorite: chocolate-flavored cookies coated with cinnamon and sugar.

Ingredients for jar:

1 ⅓ cups sugar	330 ml
1/4 cup cocoa powder	60 ml
1¾ cups flour	430 ml
½ teaspoon baking powder	2 ml
¾ cup finely chopped or ground pecans	180 ml

Instructions for jar:

1. Place sugar in 1-quart (1 L) jar and smooth over top. Gently spoon cocoa powder over sugar and even surface.

2. Spoon flour and baking powder over cocoa and press down lightly. Add pecans to jar on top of flour and press down firmly. Place lid on jar to close and attach with gift tag and directions for baking.

(Continued on next page.)

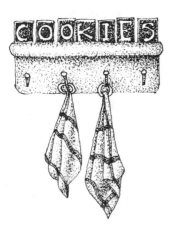

(*Continued*)

Instructions for baking:

1 egg	1
¾ cup (1½ sticks) butter, softened	180 ml
2 tablespoons milk	30 ml
1 teaspoon vanilla	5 ml
3 tablespoons sugar	45 ml
1½ teaspoons cinnamon	7 ml

1. Preheat oven to 375° (190° C). Empty contents of jar into large mixing bowl. Add egg, butter, milk and vanilla. Beat on low speed or by hand until dough thoroughly blends. Cover dough and refrigerate for 1 hour.

2. In small bowl, combine sugar and cinnamon. Stir to completely mix. Take pieces of dough and roll into 1-inch (2.5 cm) balls. Roll balls in the sugar-cinnamon mixture and place 2 inches (5 cm) apart on ungreased cookie sheet.

3. Bake for 10 to 11 minutes or until light brown around edges. Remove from oven, cool cookies on cookie sheet for 1 minute and transfer to cooling rack. Makes about 4 dozen.

Colorful Candy Cookies

Candy cookies are really sugar cookies speckled with colorful chocolate-coated candies.

Ingredients for jar:

1 cup sugar	250 ml
½ cup packed light brown sugar	125 ml
2 cups flour	500 ml
1 teaspoon baking soda	5 ml
1/4 teaspoon salt	1 ml
1 cup M&M candies	250 ml

Instructions for jar:

1. Place sugar in 1-quart (1 L) jar and smooth over top. Spoon brown sugar over top and pack down evenly.

2. In small bowl, combine flour, baking soda and salt. Stir to mix. Spoon over brown sugar in jar and press down evenly. Pour candies over flour mixture, place lid on jar and attach with gift tag and directions for baking.

Instructions for baking:

¾ cup (1½ sticks) butter, softened	180 ml
2 eggs	2

1. Preheat oven to 350° (176° C). Empty contents of jar into large bowl. Add butter and eggs. Beat by hand, so you don't break candies, until dough mixes thoroughly.

2. Drop by rounded teaspoonfuls onto ungreased cookie sheet. Bake for 10 to 12 minutes until edges brown. Remove from oven and cool cookies on cookie sheet for 1 minute, then transfer to cooling rack. Makes 3 to 3½ dozen.

Walnut-Cinnamon Balls

Powdered sugar covers these dainty little cookies that melt in your mouth. They are light and delicate and full of cinnamon flavor.

Ingredients for Jar:

¾ cup powdered sugar	180 ml
3 cups flour	750 ml
1 cup finely chopped or ground toasted walnuts*	250 ml
¼ teaspoon salt	1 ml
1 teaspoon cinnamon	5 ml

Instructions for Jar:

1. In large bowl, combine all ingredients. Stir until thoroughly mixed.

2. Fill 1-quart jar with mixture and pack down occasionally to fit it all. Place lid on jar, close and attach label with baking instructions.

To toast walnuts, spread in single layer on cookie sheet and bake at 350° (176° C) for 5 to 8 minutes or until light brown.

Instructions for Baking:

1½ cups (3 sticks) butter, softened	375 ml
1 teaspoon vanilla	5 ml
½ cup powdered sugar	125 ml

1. Preheat oven to 325° (163° C). Place butter and vanilla in large bowl. Beat on low speed and add contents of jar a little at a time, beating well after each addition.

2. Roll dough into balls 1-inch wide and place 2 inches apart on ungreased cookie sheet. Bake for 13 to 15 minutes.

3. Remove from oven and let cookies cool on cookie sheet for 1 minute, then transfer to cooling rack. Let cool for 10 minutes and then roll in powdered sugar (about ½ cup) to coat. (Makes 4 dozen.)

Toffee-Chocolate Chippers

This is a traditional chocolate chip cookie with a twist--bits of toffee scattered throughout. The cookie looks especially nice in the jar with all of its contrasting layers.

Ingredients for jar:

1/4 cup sugar	60 ml
½ cup packed light brown sugar	125 ml
1 1/4 cups flour	310 ml
1/4 teaspoon baking soda	60 ml
1 cup coarsely chopped walnuts	250 ml
1 cup semi-sweet chocolate chips	250 ml
½ cup almond toffee bits or crushed Heath bars	125 ml

Instructions for jar:

1. Pour sugar in bottom of 1-quart (1 L) jar and smooth over top. Place brown sugar on top of sugar and pack down firmly and evenly.

2. Spoon flour over brown sugar and pack down. Pour baking soda over flour. Sprinkle walnuts over flour and press down.

3. Place chocolate chips on walnuts and sprinkle toffee bits over chocolate. Press down to fit. Place lid on jar and attach with gift tag and directions for baking.

(Continued on next page.)

(Continued)

Instructions for baking:

1 egg	**1**
½ cup (1 stick) butter, softened	**125 ml**

1. Preheat oven to 375° (190° C). Empty contents of jar into large mixing bowl. Add egg and butter. Beat on low speed or by hand to blend.

2. Once dough thoroughly mixes, drop by rounded teaspoonfuls onto ungreased cookie sheet.

3. Bake for 8 to 10 minutes or until edges brown. Remove from oven and cool cookies on cookie sheet for 1 minute, then transfer to cooling rack. Makes 3 dozen.

Apricot-Angel Brownies

2 (2 ounce) bars white baking chocolate	2 (57 g)
⅓ cup butter	80 ml
⅔ cup sugar	160 ml
2 eggs, beaten	2
½ teaspoon vanilla	2 ml
¾ cup flour	180 ml
½ teaspoon baking powder	2 ml
¼ teaspoon salt	1 ml
1 cup finely chopped dried apricots	250 ml
1 (2 ounce) package sliced almonds	1 (57 g)
¼ cup flaked coconut	60 ml

1. Preheat oven to 350° (176° C).

2. In saucepan over low heat, stir and melt chocolate and butter.

3. Remove from heat and stir in sugar, eggs and vanilla. Set aside.

4. In bowl, combine flour, baking powder and salt and stir into chocolate mixture.

5. In separate bowl, combine apricots, almonds and coconut and stir about two-thirds mixture into batter.

6. In greased 7 x 11-inch (18 x 28 cm) baking dish, pour batter and sprinkle remaining apricot mixture on top.

7. Bake 25 minutes or until brownies turn golden brown. Cool.

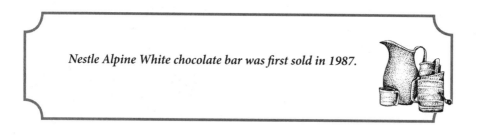

Nestle Alpine White chocolate bar was first sold in 1987.

Classic Brownies

⅔ cup oil	160 ml
2 cups sugar	500 ml
⅓ cup white corn syrup	80 ml
4 eggs, beaten	4
½ cup cocoa	125 ml
1½ cups flour	375 ml
½ teaspoon salt	2 ml
1 teaspoon baking powder	5 ml
2 teaspoons vanilla	10 ml
1 cup chopped pecans	250 ml

1. Preheat oven to 350° (176° C).

2. In mixing bowl, beat oil, sugar, corn syrup and eggs.

3. Add cocoa, flour, salt, baking powder and vanilla and beat well. Stir in pecans.

4. In greased, floured 9 x 13-inch (23 x 33 cm) baking pan, pour batter and bake 45 minutes.

Buster Brownies

⅔ cup oil	160 ml
2 cups sugar	500 ml
⅓ cup corn syrup	80 ml
3 eggs, slightly beaten	3
2 teaspoons vanilla	10 ml
½ cup cocoa	125 ml
1½ cups flour	375 ml
½ teaspoon salt	2 ml
1 teaspoon baking powder	5 ml
1 cup chopped pecans	250 ml

Frosting:

2 cups powdered sugar	500 ml
⅓ cup cocoa	80 ml
¼ cup (1 stick) butter, melted	60 ml
1 tablespoon milk	15 ml
1 teaspoon vanilla	5 ml

1. Preheat oven to 350° (176° C).

2. In mixing bowl, beat oil, sugar, corn syrup, eggs and vanilla. Add cocoa, flour, salt and baking powder and beat well. Stir in chopped pecans.

3. In 9 x 13-inch (23 x 33 cm) greased, floured baking pan, pour batter and bake 35 minutes. Brownies are done when toothpick inserted in center comes out clean. Cool.

4. To make frosting, mix powdered sugar, cocoa, butter, milk and vanilla and spread over brownies.

Chewy Caramel Brownies

50 caramels (about 14 ounces), unwrapped	50
1 (5 ounce) can evaporated milk, divided	1 (142 g)
1 (18 ounce) package German chocolate cake mix	1 (520 g)
¼ cup (½ stick) butter, melted	60 ml
1 cup chopped nuts	250 ml
1 cup semi-sweet chocolate chips	250 ml

1. Preheat oven to 350° (176° C).

2. In saucepan over low heat, melt and stir caramels with ⅓ cup (80 ml) evaporated milk.

3. In mixing bowl, combine cake mix, melted butter and remaining milk.

4. In bottom of greased 9 x 13-inch (23 x 33 cm) baking pan, spread half cake mixture and bake 7 minutes.

5. Sprinkle crust with pecans, chocolate chips and melted caramels.

6. Drop spoonfuls of remaining cake mixture over top and lightly spread with back of spoon.

7. Bake 18 to 20 minutes. Cool completely before cutting into squares. Yields about 24 brownies.

This is worth all the time it takes to unwrap those 50 caramels!

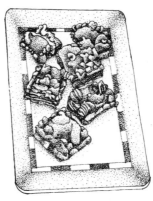

Butterscotch Brownies

3 cups packed brown sugar	750 ml
1 cup (2 sticks) butter, softened	250 ml
3 eggs	3
3 cups flour	750 ml
2 tablespoons baking powder	30 ml
½ teaspoon salt	2 ml
1½ cups chopped pecans	375 ml
1 cup flaked coconut	250 ml

Glaze:

½ cup packed brown sugar	125 ml
⅓ cup evaporated milk	80 ml
½ cup (1 stick) butter	125 ml
⅛ teaspoon salt	.5 ml
1 cup powdered sugar	250 ml
½ teaspoon vanilla	2 ml

1. Preheat oven to 350° (176° C).

2. In mixing bowl, combine and beat brown sugar and butter until fluffy. Add eggs and blend.

3. In separate bowl, sift flour, baking powder and salt and add to brown sugar mixture 1 cup (250 ml) at a time. Add pecans and coconut.

4. In well-greased 11 x 17-inch (28 x 43 cm) pan, spread batter (it will be hard to spread) and bake 20 to 25 minutes.

5. To make glaze, combine brown sugar, milk, butter and salt and bring to boil. Cool slightly, add powdered sugar and vanilla and beat until smooth.

6. Spread glaze over cooled brownies and cut in squares.

Cashew Brownies

18 caramels, unwrapped	18
6 tablespoons (¾ stick) butter	90 ml
2 tablespoons milk	30 ml
¾ cup sugar	180 ml
2 eggs, beaten	2
1 teaspoon vanilla	5 ml
1 cup flour	250 ml
½ teaspoon baking powder	2 ml
1 cup chopped salted cashews	250 ml

1. Preheat oven to 350° (176° C).

2. In saucepan over low heat, combine caramels, butter and milk and stir constantly until caramels melt and mixture is smooth.

3. Remove from heat and stir in sugar. Cool several minutes, then add eggs and vanilla.

4. In bowl, combine flour and baking powder. Stir in caramel mixture and blend. Fold in cashews.

5. In greased, floured 9-inch (23 cm) baking pan, spoon batter and bake about 25 minutes. Brownies are done when toothpick inserted in center comes out clean.

6. Cool on wire rack and cut in bars.

Grasshopper Brownies

4 (1 ounce) squares unsweetened chocolate	4 (28 g)
1 cup (2 sticks) butter	250 ml
2 cups sugar	500 ml
3 large eggs, lightly beate	3
1 cup flour	250 ml
1 teaspoon vanilla	5 ml
½ teaspoon salt	2 ml
1 cup chopped pecans	250 ml

First Icing Layer:

2 cups powdered sugar	500 ml
3 tablespoons butter, melted	45 ml
4 tablespoons green crème de menthe	60 ml
1 tablespoon milk	15 ml

Second Icing Layer:

4 (1 ounce) squares semi-sweet chocolate	4 (28 g)
4 tablespoons butter	60 ml

1. Preheat oven to 350° (176° C). In saucepan, melt chocolate and butter.

2. In mixing bowl, beat sugar and eggs. Pour in melted chocolate mixture and mix. Add flour, vanilla, salt and pecans and mix well.

3. In greased, floured 9 x 13-inch (23 x 33 cm) baking pan, pour batter and bake 30 to 35 minutes. Brownies are done when toothpick inserted in center comes out clean. Cool.

4. In separate bowl, mix powdered sugar, butter, creme de menthe and milk. Frost cooled brownies.

5. In saucepan, melt chocolate and butter. Pour over creme de menthe layer and smooth. Cut in bars to serve.

Rum-Frosted Brownies

1 cup (2 sticks) butter	250 ml
4 ounces unsweetened chocolate	115 g
3 eggs	3
2 cups sugar	500 ml
2 teaspoons vanilla	10 ml
1 cup flour	250 ml
1 cup chopped pecans	250 ml

Rum Frosting:

½ cup (1 stick) butter, softened	125 ml
1 (16 ounce) box powdered sugar	1 (454 g)
3½ tablespoons rum	52 ml
1 (6 ounces) package semi-sweet chocolate	1 (170 g)
2 tablespoons butter	30 ml
½ cup chopped pecans	125 ml

1. Preheat oven to 350° (176° C). In saucepan, melt butter and chocolate and set aside to cool.

2. In large mixing bowl, beat eggs, sugar and vanilla. Stir in chocolate mixture and gradually fold in flour. Stir in pecans.

3. In greased, floured 9 x 13-inch (23 x 33 cm) baking pan, spread batter and bake 30 minutes or until top feels firm to the touch. Cool completely.

4. In separate bowl, combine butter, powdered sugar and rum and spread over cooled brownies. Melt chocolate and butter and spread evenly over powdered sugar mixture.

5. Sprinkle ½ cup (125 ml) chopped pecans over chocolate. Let stand until chocolate becomes firm, then cut into bars.

You may substitute 3 teaspoons (15 ml) milk and
1½ teaspoons (7 ml) rum flavoring for rum.

Classic Blonde Brownies

¾ cup butter (1½ sticks) butter, softened	180 ml
1¾ cups packed light brown sugar	330 ml
3 eggs, lightly beaten	3
1 teaspoon vanilla	5 ml
2¼ cups flour	560 ml
2½ teaspoons baking powder	12 ml
½ teaspoon salt	2 ml
1 (12 ounce) package chocolate chips	1 (340 g)

1. Preheat oven to 350° (176° C). Combine butter and sugar in large bowl until creamy. Stir in eggs and vanilla and mix thoroughly.

2. Gradually add flour, baking powder and salt a little at a time and beat after each addition. Stir in chocolate chips.

3. Pour into greased 10 x 15-inch (25 x 38 cm) jelly-roll pan and bake for about 22 minutes or until top springs back. Cool in pan and cut into squares.

Quick Blonde Brownies

1 (16 ounce) box light brown sugar	1 (454 g)
4 eggs	4
2 cups buttermilk biscuit baking mix	500 ml
2 cups chopped pecans	500 ml

1. Preheat oven to 350° (176° C).

2. In mixing bowl, mix brown sugar, eggs and baking mix. Stir in pecans.

3. In greased 9 x 13-inch (23 x 33 cm) baking pan, pour batter and bake 35 minutes. Cool and cut in squares.

So easy and so very good!

In-a-Rush Brownies

2 cups graham cracker crumbs	500 ml
1 (14 ounce) can sweetened condensed milk	1 (420 g)
1 (6 ounce) package chocolate chips	1 (170 g)
1 cup chopped pecans	250 ml
⅛ teaspoon salt	.5 ml

1. Preheat oven to 350° (176° C). In mixing bowl, combine all ingredients and mix well.

2. Grease 8-inch (20 cm) square cake pan. Spoon batter into pan.

3. Bake 40 minutes. Immediately cut into squares and remove from pan. Cool.

Classic Magic Cookie Bars

½ cup (1 stick) butter	125 ml
1⅔ cups graham cracker crumbs	410 ml
1½ cups flaked coconut	375 ml
1 (6 ounce) package semi-sweet chocolate chips	1 (170 g)
1 (6 ounce) package butterscotch chips	1 (170 g)
1½ cups chopped pecans	375 ml
1 (14 ounce) can sweetened condensed milk	1 (420 g)

1. Preheat oven to 325° (163° C).

2. In 9-inch (23 cm) square pan, place butter and bake just until it melts.

3. Add layer of graham cracker crumbs, layer of coconut, layer of chocolate chips, layer of butterscotch chips and layer of pecans. Do not stir.

4. Slowly pour condensed milk evenly over pecans. Bake about 30 minutes.

5. Cool completely before cutting in squares.

Iced Chocolate Chip Bars

2 eggs	2
1 teaspoon vanilla	5 ml
⅓ cup oil	80 ml
1 (18 ounce) package yellow cake mix	1 (520 g)
1¼ cups semi-sweet chocolate chips	310 ml
¾ cup chopped pecans	180 ml

1. Preheat oven to 375° (190° C).

2. In mixing bowl, combine eggs, vanilla, oil and cake mix and beat until smooth and fluffy. Stir in chocolate chips and pecans.

3. In 9 x 13-inch (23 x 33 cm) baking dish, press batter evenly with spatula or fingers and bake 30 minutes.

4. Frost with Zippy Chocolate Frosting.

Zippy Chocolate Frosting:

1 (16 ounce) box powdered sugar	1 (454 g)
⅓ cup cocoa	80 ml
1 teaspoon vanilla	5 ml
3 tablespoons melted butter	45 ml
⅓ cup coffee, hot or cold	80 ml

1. In mixing bowl, combine all ingredients and mix well.

2. Immediately frost bars.

Chocolate-Cheesecake Bars

2 (16 ounce) rolls refrigerated chocolate chip cookie dough	2 (454 g)
4 (8 ounce) package cream cheese, softened	4 (228 g)
2 eggs, beaten	2
2 cups sugar	500 ml
1 teaspoon vanilla	5 ml

1. Preheat oven to 350° (176° C).

2. Thinly slice one roll cookie dough. On bottom of 9 x 13-inch (23 x 33 cm) baking pan, place slices and press together to form crust.

3. In mixing bowl with electric mixer, beat cream cheese, eggs, sugar and vanilla and spread over cookie dough slices.

4. Slice second roll cookie dough and place slices over creamed mixture.

5. Bake 25 to 30 minutes and cool before slicing.

Cream cheese was introduced in 1880 by the Phenix Cheese Company and named Philadelphia Brand Cream Cheese. Phenix was purchased by the Kraft Cheese Company in 1928.

Butter-Pecan Turtle Bars

2 cups flour	500 ml
1¾ cups packed light brown sugar, divided	430 ml
1¼ cups (2½ sticks) butter, softened, divided	310 ml
1½ cups coarsely chopped pecans	375 ml
5 (1 ounce) squares semi-sweet chocolate	5 (28 g)
¼ cup (½ stick) butter	60 ml

1. Preheat oven to 350° (176° C).

2. In large mixing bowl, combine flour, ¾ cup (180 ml) packed brown sugar and ½ cup (125 ml) butter and blend until crumbly.

3. In greased 9 x 13-inch (23 x 33 cm) baking pan, pat mixture firmly and sprinkle pecans over unbaked crust. Set aside.

4. In small saucepan over medium heat, combine 1 cup (250 ml) packed brown sugar and remaining ¾ cup (180 ml) butter and stir constantly until mixture boils. Cook and stir 1 minute.

5. Drizzle caramel sauce over pecans and crust.

6. Bake 18 minutes or until caramel layer bubbles. Remove from oven and cool.

7. In saucepan, melt chocolate squares and ¼ cup (60 ml) butter and stir until smooth. Pour over bars and spread evenly.

8. Cool and cut into bars. Store in refrigerator.

Baby Ruth Bars

1 cup light corn syrup	250 ml
1 cup sugar	250 ml
1½ cups chunky peanut butter	375 ml
4½ to 5 cups crispy rice cereal	1 L to 1 L + 250 ml
1 (12 ounce) package chocolate chips	1 (340 g)
½ bar paraffin	½

1. In medium saucepan, bring corn syrup and sugar to full boil.

2. Remove from heat, add peanut butter and mix. Add cereal and mix.

3. Form mixture in bars about 2 to 3 inches long.

4. In smaller saucepan, melt chocolate chips and paraffin.

5. Dip logs in paraffin mixture by using toothpicks to pick up bars.

6. Make sure bars are completely dry before storing.

Peanut butter was first made in 1890.

Death-By-Chocolate Bars

1 cup (2 sticks) butter, softened	250 ml
2 cups sugar	500 ml
1 tablespoon vanilla	15 ml
4 eggs	4
1½ cups flour	375 ml
½ cup cocoa	125 ml
1½ cups chopped pecans	375 ml
1 (7 ounce) jar marshmallow cream	1 (198 g)

Frosting:

½ cup (1 stick) butter	125 ml
2 tablespoons milk	30 ml
3 tablespoons cocoa	45 ml
3 cups powdered sugar	750 ml

1. Preheat oven to 350° (176° C).

2. In mixing bowl, combine butter, sugar, vanilla and eggs and beat 3 minutes.

3. Add flour and cocoa and beat until ingredients mix well. Stir in pecans.

4. In greased, floured 9 x 13-inch (23 x 33 cm) baking pan, bake 40 minutes. Bars are done when toothpick inserted in center comes out clean.

5. Immediately spread marshmallow cream over hot cake and set aside to cool.

6. To make frosting, combine butter, milk, cocoa and powdered sugar in mixing bowl and mix well. Spread over marshmallow cream.

Chocolate Rocky Roads

1 (18 ounce) package double chocolate chunk cookie mix	**1 (520 g)**
1⅓ cups oil	**330 ml**
2 tablespoons water	**30 ml**
1 egg, beaten	**1**
½ (16 ounce) carton ready-to-spread chocolate frosting	**228 g**
½ cup miniature marshmallows	**125 ml**
¼ cup chopped peanuts	**60 ml**

1. Preheat oven to 350° (176° C).

2. In mixing bowl, combine cookie mix, oil, water and egg and mix until dough forms.

3. In ungreased 8 x 8-inch (20 x 20 cm) square baking pan, press dough and bake 20 to 25 minutes or until center sets. Cool.

4. In separate bowl, combine frosting and marshmallows and spread over bars. Sprinkle with chopped peanuts.

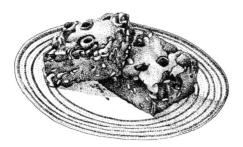

Easy Chocolate Chip Bars

1 cup (2 sticks) butter, softened	250 ml
1½ cups packed brown sugar	375 ml
1 egg, beaten	1
2 teaspoons vanilla	10 ml
2 cups flour	500 ml
1 (16 ounce) package milk chocolate chips	1 (454 g)
¾ cup chopped pecans	180 ml

1. Preheat oven to 350° (176° C).

2. In mixing bowl, beat butter, brown sugar, egg and vanilla.

3. Fold in remaining ingredients and mix well.

4. In greased 9 x 13-inch (23 x 33 cm) baking pan, spoon batter and bake 20 minutes or until tops brown lightly.

5. Cool and cut into bars.

*N*estle Chocolate Company originally sold a mini-chocolate chopper with its chocolate bars so customers could make Ruth Wakefield's cookie recipe.

Classic Candy Bars

1 cup (2 sticks) butter	250 ml
1 cup packed light brown sugar	250 ml
1 cup packed dark brown sugar	250 ml
1 egg yolk	1
1 teaspoon vanilla	5 ml
2 cups flour	500 ml
¼ teaspoon salt	1 ml
16 (1.2 ounce) chocolate bars	16 (30 g)

1. Preheat oven to 350° (176° C).

2. In mixing bowl, combine butter, both sugars, egg yolk and vanilla and mix well.

3. Fold in flour and salt and mix well. In greased 9 x 13-inch (23 x 33 cm) baking pan, pour batter and bake 20 minutes.

4. Remove from oven and top immediately with chocolate bars. When chocolate melts, spread with knife to cover. Cool and cut into bars.

Hershey bars were first produced in 1894.

Fudge-Oat Bars

2 cups quick-cooking oats	500 ml
1½ cups flour	375 ml
1 cup packed light brown sugar	250 ml
1 cup (2 sticks) butter, melted	250 ml
1 cup chopped walnuts	250 ml
1 (14 ounce) can sweetened condensed milk	1 (420 g)
1 (6 ounce) package milk chocolate chips	1 (170 g)
1 cup plain M&M candies	250 ml

1. Preheat oven to 350° (176° C).

2. In bowl, combine oats, flour and brown sugar. Cut in butter until it resembles coarse crumbs and stir in walnuts.

3. Set aside 1½ cups (375 ml) for topping and press remaining crumb mixture into greased 9 x 13-inch (23 x 33 cm) baking dish.

4. In saucepan, combine condensed milk and chocolate chips. Cook and stir over low heat until chips melt.

5. Spread over crust and sprinkle with 1½ cups (375 ml) crumbs saved for topping.

6. Top with M&M candies and bake for 20 to 25 minutes or until edges are light brown. Cool and cut into bars.

Chunky Oatmeal Bars

¾ cup (1½ sticks) butter, softened	180 ml
1 cup packed light brown sugar	250 ml
⅓ cup light corn syrup	80 ml
1 ½ teaspoons vanilla	7 ml
4 cups oats	1 L
1 (12 ounce) package milk chocolate chips	1 (340 g)
¾ cup creamy peanut butter	180 ml
1 (12 ounce) package butter brickle chips	1 (340 g)

1. Preheat oven to 350° (176° C).

2. In mixing bowl, combine butter, brown sugar, corn syrup and vanilla and beat well.

3. Stir in oats and press into buttered 9 x 13-inch (23 x 33 cm) baking dish.

4. Bake for 13 to 14 minutes, or until golden brown. Cool on wire rack.

5. In heavy saucepan, melt chocolate chips and peanut butter and stir until blended. Spread over cooled bars and sprinkle with butter brickle chips.

6. Refrigerate several hours or overnight until set before cutting into bars.

World's Best Bars

¾ cup (1½ sticks) butter, softened	180 ml
1½ cups packed brown sugar	375 ml
½ cup white corn syrup	125 ml
1 tablespoon vanilla	15 ml
4 cups oats	1 L
1 (6 ounce) package butterscotch chips	1 (170 g)
¼ cup peanut butter	60 ml

1. Preheat oven to 350° (176° C).

2. In bowl combine butter, brown sugar, corn syrup, vanilla and oats. Beat until ingredients blend well.

3. In greased 9 x 13-inch (23 x 33 cm) baking pan, pat dough and bake 15 minutes or until top browns lightly. Cool 10 minutes.

4. In saucepan, heat butterscotch chips and peanut butter and stir until chips melt. Spread over top.

5. Cool before cutting in bars.

The Karo Company touts the creation of the recipe for corn syrup with the wife of their corporate sales executive in the 1930's.

Butterscotch-Cheesecake Bars

1 (12 ounce) package butterscotch chips	1 (340 g)
⅓ cup (5 tablespoons) butter	80 ml
2 cups graham cracker crumbs	500 ml
1 cup chopped pecans	250 ml
1 (8 ounce) package cream cheese, softened	1 (228 g)
1 (14 ounce) can sweetened condensed milk	1 (420 g)
1½ teaspoons vanilla	7 ml
1 egg	1

1. Preheat oven to 350° (176° C).

2. In large saucepan, melt butterscotch chips and butter and mix well. Add crumbs and pecans and mix well.

3. In bottom of greased, floured 9 x 13-inch (23 x 33 cm) baking pan, firmly press half mixture. Reserve other half and set aside.

4. In mixing bowl, beat cream cheese, condensed milk, vanilla and egg until smooth. Pour over crumb mixture and top with remaining crumb mixture.

5. Bake 25 to 30 minutes or until center sets. Chill before cutting into bars. Store in refrigerator.

Chewy Butterscotch Bars

1 cup packed brown sugar	250 ml
½ cup (1 stick) butter, softened	125 ml
2 eggs	2
1 teaspoon vanilla	5 ml
½ cup flour	125 ml
1 (3.75 ounce) package instant butterscotch	
pudding mix	1 (100 g)
¼ teaspoon salt	1 ml
¾ cup quick-cooking oats	180 ml
Powdered sugar	

1. Preheat oven to 350° (176° C).

2. In mixing bowl, beat sugar and butter. Add eggs and vanilla and beat well.

3. In separate bowl, mix flour, dry pudding mix and salt. Add to sugar mixture and mix well. Stir in oats and mix.

4. In greased, floured 9 x 9-inch (23 x 23 cm) baking pan, spread batter and bake 30 to 35 minutes. Bars are done when toothpick inserted in center comes out clean. Cool in pan.

5. With shaker or sifter, sprinkle powdered sugar over top of mixture. Cut into bars.

Classic Million Dollar Bars

½ cup (1 stick) butter	125 ml
2 cups graham cracker crumbs	500 ml
1 (6 ounce) package chocolate chips	1 (170 g)
1 (6 ounce) package butterscotch chips	1 (170 g)
1 cup chopped pecans	250 ml
1 (7 ounce) can flaked coconut	1 (198 g)
1 (14 ounce) can sweetened condensed milk	1 (420 g)

1. Preheat oven to 325° (163° C).

2. In 9 x 13-inch (23 x 33 cm) ovenproof glass baking dish, melt butter. Sprinkle crumbs over butter and stir.

3. In bottom of baking dish, spread mixture evenly to form crust.

4. Add layers of chocolate chips, butterscotch chips, pecans and

Baker's chocolate was developed in 1764.

Almond-Butter Bars

1 cup (2 sticks) butter, softened	250 ml
2 cups sugar	500 ml
3 eggs, beaten	3
2 cups flour	500 ml
1½ teaspoons baking powder	7 ml
3½ teaspoons almond extract	17 ml
½ cup finely chopped slivered almonds	125 ml

1. Preheat oven to 350° (176° C).

2. In mixing bowl, combine butter and sugar and beat until fluffy. Add eggs and beat thoroughly.

3. In separate bowl, combine flour and baking powder and gradually add to sugar mixture.

4. Fold in almond extract and chopped slivered almonds and mix well.

5. In greased, floured 9 x 13-inch (23 x 33 cm) baking pan, spread dough and bake 35 minutes. Cool and cut into bars.

Be sure to use butter. There is no substitute
for the real thing in this recipe.

Almond-Coconut Squares

2 cups graham cracker crumbs	500 ml
3 tablespoons brown sugar	45 ml
½ cup (1 stick) butter, melted	125 ml
1 (14 ounce) can sweetened condensed milk	1 (420 g)
1 (7 ounce) package flaked coconut	1 (198 g)
1 teaspoon vanilla	5 ml

Topping:

1 (6 ounce) package chocolate chips	1 (170 g)
1 (6 ounce) package butterscotch chips	1 (170 g)
4 tablespoons butter	60 ml
6 tablespoons chunky peanut butter	90 ml
½ cup slivered almonds	125 ml

1. Preheat oven to 325° (163° C).

2. In mixing bowl, combine graham cracker crumbs, brown sugar and butter.

3. In greased 9 x 13-inch (23 x 33 cm) baking pan, pat mixture and bake 10 minutes. Cool.

4. In bowl, combine sweetened condensed milk, coconut and vanilla. Pour over baked crust and bake another 25 minutes. Cool.

5. To make topping, combine all topping ingredients in top of double boiler, heat and stir until chips melt. Spread over baked ingredients.

6. Cool and cut into squares. Makes 3 dozen.

Almond-Crisp Squares

4 eggs	4
2 cups sugar	500 ml
1 cup (2 sticks) butter, melted	250 ml
2 cups flour	500 ml
2 teaspoons almond extract	10 ml
⅔ cup slivered almonds	160 ml
Powdered sugar for garnish	

1. Preheat oven to 325° (163° C).

2. In mixing bowl, beat eggs and sugar until lemon colored. Add melted butter, flour, almond extract and almonds and mix well.

3. Spread into buttered 9 x 13-inch (23 x 33 cm) baking dish.

4. Bake for 30 to 35 minutes or until toothpick inserted near center comes out clean.

5. Cool, cut into squares and sprinkle with powdered sugar.

A cookie sheet is a rectangle pan about 14 x 16 inches with no sides. A baking sheet is a rectangle pan about 10 x 15 inches with 1-inch sides. A 9 x 13-inch baking pan has sides 2 to 3 inches high.

Almond-Fudge Shortbread

1 cup (2 sticks) butter, softened	250 ml
½ cup powdered sugar	125 ml
¼ teaspoon salt	1 ml
1½ cups flour	375 ml
1 (12 ounce) package chocolate chips	1 (340 g)
1 (14 ounce) can sweetened condensed milk	1 (420 g)
½ teaspoon almond extract	2 ml
1 (2.5 ounce) package almonds, toasted	1 (70 g)

1. Preheat oven to 350° (176° C). Grease 9 x 13-inch (23 x 33 cm) baking pan.

2. In mixing bowl, beat butter, sugar and salt. Stir in flour. Pat in prepared pan and bake 15 minutes.

3. In medium saucepan over low heat, melt chocolate chips with sweetened condensed milk and stir constantly until chips melt.

4. Stir in almond extract and spread evenly over shortbread. Sprinkle with almonds.

5. Refrigerate several hours or until firm and cut into bars. Store at room temperature.

Classic Pecan Tassies

½ cup butter, softened	125 ml
1 (3 ounce) package cream cheese, softened	1 (85 g)
1 cup flour	250 ml
2/3 cup crushed pecans	160 ml
1 egg	1
¾ cup packed brown sugar	180 ml
1 tablespoon butter, softened	15 ml
1 teaspoon vanilla	5 ml
Dash salt	

1. Cream ½ cup (125 ml) butter and cream cheese until smooth. Stir in flour and blend well. Chill dough about 1 hour.

2. Preheat oven to 325° (163° C). Make 1-inch balls and place in ungreased, miniature muffin cups. Press dough in bottom and sides to form crust. Place half of pecans in muffin cups.

3. Beat egg, brown sugar, 1 tablespoon (15 ml) butter, vanilla and salt until smooth. Pour filling mixture into muffin cups and top with remaining pecans.

4. Bake for about 25 minutes or until filling sets. Cool and remove from pan.

Pecan Chewies

3 eggs, beaten	3
1 (16 ounce) box light brown sugar	1 (454 g)
1 teaspoon vanilla	5 ml
½ cup (1 stick) butter, melted, slightly cooled	125 ml
2 cups flour	500 ml
2 teaspoons baking powder	10 ml
1½ cups chopped pecans	375 ml

1. Preheat oven to 350° (176° C).

2. In mixing bowl, combine eggs, brown sugar, vanilla and butter and mix well.

3. Gradually add flour and baking powder and blend well. Fold in pecans.

4. Grease and flour 9 x 13-inch (23 x 33 cm) baking pan and spread batter in pan.

5. Bake 35 minutes and check center for doneness. If center is sticky, bake 4 to 5 minutes longer.

6. Cool and cut in squares.

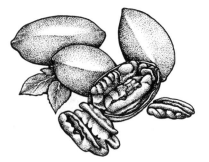

Pecan Cream Cheese Squares

1 (18 ounce) package yellow cake mix	1 (520 g)
3 eggs, divided	3
½ cup (1 stick) butter, softened	125 ml
2 cups chopped pecans	500 ml
1 (8 ounce) package cream cheese, softened	1 (228 g)
3⅔ cups powdered sugar	910 ml

1. Preheat oven to 350° (176° C).

2. In mixing bowl, combine cake mix, 1 egg and butter.

3. Stir in pecans and mix well.

4. In greased 9 x 13-inch (23 x 33 cm) baking pan, press mixture evenly.

5. In mixing bowl, beat cream cheese, sugar and remaining eggs until smooth. Pour over pecan mixture.

6. Bake 55 minutes or until top turns golden brown.

7. Cool and cut in squares.

Cream cheese was introduced in 1880 by the Phenix Cheese Company and named Philadelphia Brand Cream Cheese. Phenix was purchased by the Kraft Cheese Company in 1928.

Pecan Pie Squares

Crust:

3 cups flour	750 ml
¾ (1½ sticks) butter, softened	180 ml
⅓ cup sugar	80 ml
¾ teaspoon salt	4 ml

Filling:

4 eggs, beaten	4
1½ cups packed brown sugar	375 ml
1½ cups light corn syrup	375 ml
3 tablespoons butter, melted	45 ml
1½ teaspoons vanilla	7 ml
2½ cups chopped pecans	625 ml

1. Preheat oven to 350° (176° C).

2. In mixing bowl with electric mixer, blend flour, butter, sugar and salt.

3. In greased 12 x 18-inch (30 x 46 cm) jelly-roll pan, press dough and bake 25 minutes or until crust browns.

4. In same bowl, combine eggs, brown sugar, corn syrup, butter and vanilla and mix well. Spread pecans over crust, then pour egg mixture over baked layer and spread evenly.

5. Bake about 25 minutes more or until filling sets.

6. Cool and cut in squares.

Classic Peanut Dream Bars

2 cups quick-cooking oats	500 ml
1½ cups flour	375 ml
1 cup chopped peanuts	250 ml
1 cup packed brown sugar	250 ml
1 teaspoon baking soda	5 ml
½ teaspoon salt	2 ml
1 cup (2 sticks) butter, melted	250 ml
1 (14 ounce) can sweetened condensed milk	1 (420 g)
½ cup peanut butter	125 ml
1 cup M&M candies	250 ml

1. Preheat oven to 350° (176° C).

2. In mixing bowl, combine oats, flour, peanuts, sugar, baking soda and salt and mix well.

3. Add butter and mix until mixture resembles coarse crumbs. Reserve 1½ cups (375 ml) crumb mixture.

4. In bottom of greased 15 x 10-inch (38 x 25 cm) jelly-roll pan, press remaining mixture and bake 12 minutes.

5. In same mixing bowl, combine sweetened condensed milk and peanut butter and mix.

6. Spread condensed milk mixture over partially baked crust to within ¼ inch (.5 cm) from edge.

7. Combine reserved crumb mixture and candy and sprinkle evenly over condensed milk mixture. Press in lightly.

8. Bake another 20 to 22 minutes or until top turns golden brown. Cool before cutting in bars.

Peanutty Squares

4 cups bite-size crispy corn cereal	1 L
1 cup light corn syrup	250 ml
1¼ cups sugar	310 ml
1 cup creamy peanut butter	250 ml
1¼ cups salted peanuts	310 ml
2 teaspoons vanilla	10 ml

1. Place corn cereal in large bowl. In saucepan, combine corn syrup and sugar, bring to boil and boil 1 minute. Remove from heat, stir in peanut butter and blend well. Stir in peanuts and vanilla, pour over cereal and mix lightly. Spoon into buttered 9 x 13-inch (23 x 33 cm) dish. Cool and cut into squares.

Rhubarb Bars

3 cups rhubarb, cut into pieces	750 ml
1½ cups sugar	375 ml
2 tablespoons cornstarch	30 ml
¼ cup water	60 ml
1½ cups flour	375 ml
1 cup brown sugar	250 ml
½ teaspoon baking soda	2 ml
1 cup shortening	250 ml
1 teaspoon vanilla	5 ml
½ cup nuts	125 ml
1½ cups oatmeal	375 ml

1. Preheat oven to 375° (190° C). Dissolve cornstarch in water. Combine rhubarb, sugar and vanilla and cook until mixture thickens. Combine oatmeal, flour, brown sugar, baking soda, shortening and nuts until mixture crumbles. Press ¾ dry mixture into 9 x 13-inch (23 x 33 cm) pan. Pour cooled rhubarb mixture and sprinkle remaining crumbs on top. Bake for 30 to 35 minutes.

Peanut Bars

1 (18 ounce) package yellow cake mix	1 (520 g)
1 cup crunchy peanut butter, divided	250 ml
1 egg	1
1 (8 ounce) package cream cheese, softened	1 (228 g)
⅓ cup milk	80 ml
½ cup sugar	125 ml
1 (6 ounce) package milk chocolate chips	1 (170 g)
1 cup salted peanuts	250 ml

1. Preheat oven to 350° (176° C).

2. In mixing bowl, beat cake mix, ⅔ cup (160 ml) peanut butter and egg until crumbly. Press into greased 9 x 13-inch (23 x 33 cm) baking pan.

3. In mixing bowl, combine cream cheese and remaining peanut butter. Gradually beat in milk and sugar.

4. Carefully spread over crust and sprinkle with chocolate chips and peanuts.

5. Bake for 25 minutes or until edges are light brown. Cool and store in refrigerator after cutting into bars.

Joseph L. Rosefield began marketing a smooth, non-separating peanut butter in California in 1922 and partnered with Swift & Company to improve its E.K. Pond peanut butter (changed to "Peter Pan" in 1928). Later Rosefield had a disagreement with Swift and started his own peanut butter brand, Skippy.

Macadamia Nut Bars

Pastry:

½ cup (1 stick) butter, softened	125 ml
¼ cup sugar	60 ml
1 cup flour	250 ml

Topping:

2 eggs	2
1⅔ cups packed brown sugar	410 ml
2 tablespoons flour	30 ml
1 teaspoon vanilla	5 ml
½ teaspoon salt	2 ml
¼ teaspoon baking powder	1 ml
½ cup flaked coconut	2 ml
1 cup chopped macadamia nuts	250 ml

Frosting:

3 tablespoons butter, softened	45 ml
1½ cups powdered sugar	375 ml
1½ to 2 tablespoons milk	22 to 37 ml
Chopped macadamia nuts	

1. Preheat oven to 350° (176° C).

2. In mixing bowl, cream butter and sugar. Gradually add flour until pastry becomes smooth.

3. In bottom of greased 9-inch (23 cm) baking pan, pat dough and bake 18 minutes.

4. In same mixing bowl, combine eggs, sugar, flour, vanilla, salt and baking powder. Fold in coconut and macadamia nuts.

5. Spread mixture over pastry and return to oven 20 minutes more or until it feels firm to the touch. Cool.

(Continued on next page.)

(Continued)

6. To make frosting, combine butter, powdered sugar and milk in separate bowl.

7. When bars are completely cool, spread with frosting and sprinkle with chopped macadamia nuts.   Cut in squares.

Peanut Butter Bars

1 (18 ounce) package yellow cake mix	1 (520 g)
3 eggs, beaten	3
1 cup chunky peanut butter	250 ml
½ cup (1 stick) butter, melted	125 ml
1 (6 ounce) package peanut butter chips	1 (170 g)
1 (14 ounce) can sweetened condensed milk	1 (420 g)
½ cup chopped peanuts	125 ml

1. Preheat oven to 350° (176° C).

2. In mixing bowl, combine cake mix, eggs, peanut butter and butter and beat at medium speed about 2 minutes. (Mixture will be thick.)

3. In ungreased 9 x 13-inch (23 x 33 cm) baking pan, press half mixture and set aside remaining half.

4. Bake 10 minutes. Remove from oven, sprinkle with peanut butter chips and drizzle with condensed milk.

5. In medium bowl, combine remaining cake mix mixture and peanuts and add to pan. Bake 30 minutes, cool and cut in bars.

Classic Applesauce Bars

1 cup sugar	250 ml
½ cup shortening	125 ml
1 egg, beaten	1
1 teaspoon vanilla	5 ml
2 cups flour	500 ml
2 teaspoons baking soda	10 ml
½ teaspoon cinnamon	2 ml
½ teaspoon cloves or nutmeg	2 ml
½ teaspoon salt	1 ml
1½ cups applesauce	375 ml
1 cup dates or raisins	250 ml
1 cup chopped nuts, chopped	250 ml

1. Preheat oven to 350° (176° C). Cream sugar and shortening. Add egg and vanilla and mix well.

2. In separate bowl, sift flour, salt, cinnamon and cloves or nutmeg. Add flour mixture a little at a time, alternating with applesauce. Mix well. Stir in dates and nuts.

3. Pour into 10 x 15-inch (25 x 38 cm) baking pan and bake for about 15 to 25 minutes. Frost with Brown sugar frosting.

Brown Sugar Frosting:

3 tablespoons sugar	45 ml
3 tablespoons brown sugar	45 ml
2 tablespoons butter	30 ml
¼ cup milk	60 ml
5 marshmallows	5
1 teaspoon vanilla	5 ml
Powdered sugar	

1. Mix all ingredients in saucepan and boil for 2 minutes. Stir in marshmallows, vanilla and powdered sugar to reach spreading consistency.

Apple-Walnut Squares

½ cup (1 stick) butter, softened	125 ml
1 cup sugar	250 ml
1 egg	1
1 cup flour	250 ml
½ teaspoon baking powder	2 ml
½ teaspoon baking soda	2 ml
½ teaspoon ground cinnamon	2 ml
1 tart apple, peeled, chopped	1
¾ cup chopped walnuts	180 ml

1. Preheat oven to 350° (176° C).

2. In mixing bowl with electric mixer, cream butter and sugar. Add egg.

3. In separate bowl, combine flour, baking powder, baking soda and cinnamon.

4. Gradually add to sugar mixture and beat just until combined. Stir in apple and walnuts.

5. In greased 7 x 11-inch (18 x 28 cm) baking dish, pour batter and bake 35 to 40 minutes.

6. Squares are done when toothpick inserted in center comes out clean. Cool on wire rack.

Caramel-Apple Squares

1¾ cups flour	430 ml
1 cup quick-cooking oats	250 ml
½ cup packed brown sugar	125 ml
½ teaspoon baking soda	2 ml
½ teaspoon salt	2 ml
1 cup (2 sticks) butter, softened	250 ml
1 cup chopped walnuts	250 ml
24 caramels, unwrapped	24
1 (14 ounce) can sweetened condensed milk	1 (420 g)
1 (21 ounce) can apple pie filling	1 (590 g)

1. Preheat oven to 350° (176° C).

2. In large bowl, combine flour, oats, brown sugar, baking soda and salt. Cut in butter until crumbly. Set aside 1½ cups (375 ml) crumb mixture.

3. On bottom of 9 x 13-inch (23 x 33 cm) baking pan, press remaining crumb mixture and bake 15 minutes.

4. Add walnuts to reserved crumb mixture.

5. In heavy saucepan over low heat, melt caramels with sweetened condensed milk and stir until smooth.

6. Spoon apple pie filling over baked crust and spread out. Pour and smooth caramel mixture over apples.

7. Sprinkle reserved crumb mixture over top. Bake another 20 minutes and cut into squares.

8. Serve warm or at room temperature with scoop of vanilla ice cream.

Apricot Squares

1½ cups flour   375 ml
1 teaspoon baking powder   5 ml
¼ teaspoon salt   1 ml
1½ cups quick-cooking oats   375 ml
1¼ cups packed brown sugar   310 ml
¾ cup (1½ sticks) butter   180 ml
1¼ cups apricot jam   310 ml

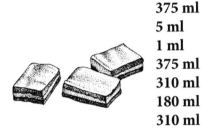

1. Preheat oven to 350° (176° C).

2. In large mixing bowl, mix flour, baking powder, salt, oats and brown sugar. Cut in butter until very crumbly.

3. In greased 9 x 13-inch (23 x 33 cm) baking pan, pat two-thirds crumb mixture.

4. Spread with jam and sprinkle remaining crumbs on top.

5. Bake 35 minutes and cool before cutting.

*F*ig Newtons and Quaker Oats Company were created in 1891.

Apricot-Almond Bars

1 (18 ounce) package yellow cake mix	1 (520 g)
½ cup (1 stick) butter, melted	125 ml
¾ cup finely chopped almonds	180 ml
1 (12 ounce) jar apricot preserves, divided	1 (340 g)
1 (8 ounce) package cream cheese, softened	1 (228 g)
¼ cup sugar	60 ml
2 tablespoons flour	30 ml
⅛ teaspoon salt	.5 ml
1 egg	1
1 teaspoon vanilla	5 ml
⅔ cup flaked coconut	160 ml

1. Preheat oven to 350°(176° C).

2. In large bowl, combine cake mix and butter and mix by hand just until crumbly. Stir in almonds and set aside 1 cup (250 ml) crumb mixture.

3. In greased 9 x 13-inch (23 x 33 cm) baking pan, lightly press remaining crumb mixture.

4. Warm 1 cup preserves and carefully spread over crumb mixture, leaving ¼-inch (.5 cm) border.

5. In mixing bowl with electric mixer, beat cream cheese until smooth. Add remaining preserves, sugar, flour, salt, egg and vanilla and beat well.

6. Carefully spread cream cheese mixture over top of preserves.

7. In separate bowl, combine 1 cup (250 ml) reserved crumb mixture and coconut and mix well. Sprinkle over cream cheese mixture.

8. Bake 35 minutes or until center sets. Cool and store in refrigerator.

Banana Bars

½ cup (1 stick) butter, softened	125 ml
1 ¾ cups sugar	430 ml
2 eggs, beaten	2
1 (8 ounce) carton sour cream	1 (228 g)
1 teaspoon vanilla	5 ml
2 cups flour	500 ml
1 teaspoon baking soda	5 ml
⅛ teaspoon salt	.5 ml
2 large bananas, mashed	2

Frosting:

1 (8 ounce) package cream cheese, softened	1 (228 g)
½ cup (1 stick) butter, softened	125 ml
2 teaspoons vanilla	10 ml
1 (16 ounce) package powdered sugar	1 (454 g)

1. Preheat oven to 350° (176° C).

2. In mixing bowl, beat butter and sugar until fluffy. Add eggs, sour cream and vanilla.

3. In separate bowl, combine flour, baking soda and salt and gradually add to sugar mixture. Fold in mashed bananas.

4. In greased, floured 10 x 15-inch (25 x 38 cm) baking pan, spoon batter and bake 20 to 25 minutes. Bars are done when toothpick inserted in center comes out clean. Cool.

5. To make frosting, beat cream cheese, butter and vanilla in mixing bowl. Gradually beat in enough powdered sugar to give frosting spreading consistency. (You may not need all the sugar.)

6. Frost bars and store in refrigerator.

Coconut-Cherry Squares

Pastry:

1⅓ cups flour	330 ml
⅝ cup (1¼ sticks) butter, softened	150 ml
1½ cups powdered sugar	375 ml

Filling:

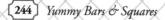

3 eggs, beaten	3
1½ cups sugar	375 ml
¾ cup flour	180 ml
½ teaspoon salt	2 ml
¾ teaspoon baking powder	4 ml
1 teaspoon vanilla	5 ml
¾ cup chopped pecans	180 ml
¾ cup flaked coconut	180 ml
¾ cup maraschino cherries, drained, chopped	180 ml

1. Preheat oven to 350° (176° C).

2. In mixing bowl, combine flour, butter and powdered sugar.

3. In bottom of 9 x 13-inch (23 x 33 cm) baking pan, press dough to form crust.

4. Bake 20 minutes or just until dough turns golden. Set aside.

5. Using same mixing bowl, combine filling ingredients and mix well. Spread over crust.

6. Bake 25 minutes or until top turns golden brown. Cool and cut in squares.

Give this recipe a festive holiday look by using half green and half red maraschino cherries.

Cranberry Bars

1½ cups vanilla wafer crumbs	375 ml
½ cup (1 stick) butter, melted	125 ml
1 (12 ounce) package white chocolate chips	1 (340 g)
1½ cups dried craisins (sweetened dried cranberries)	375 ml
1 (14 ounce) can sweetened condensed milk	1 (420 g)
1 cup chopped pecans	250 ml
1 (7 ounce) can flaked coconut	1 (198 g)

1. Preheat oven to 350° (176° C).

2. Combine vanilla wafer crumbs and melted butter and press into buttered 9 x 13-inch (23 x 33 cm) baking dish.

3. In bowl, combine white chocolate chips, craisins, condensed milk, pecans and coconut. Spread craisin mixture over vanilla wafer crust.

4. Bake for about 20 to 25 minutes or until edges are light brown. Cool and cut into bars.

G irl Scout cookies were first sold in 1936.

Classic Lemon Bars

1 cup (2 sticks) butter	250 ml
2 cups flour	500 ml
½ cup powdered sugar	125 ml
2 cups sugar	500 ml
6 tablespoons flour	90 ml
4 eggs, beaten	4
6 tablespoons lemon juice	90 ml
Grated rind of 1 lemon	1
Powdered sugar	

1. Preheat oven to 350°.

2. In 9 x 13-inch (23 x 33 cm) baking pan, place butter and melt in oven.

3. In medium bowl, combine 2 cups (500 ml) flour and powdered sugar and stir into melted butter.

4. In baking pan, press dough evenly and firmly and bake 20 minutes or until top turns golden brown.

5. In mixing bowl, combine sugar and 6 tablespoons flour. Add eggs, lemon juice and lemon rind. Mix and pour over crust.

6. Bake another 20 minutes, then cool and dust with powdered sugar.

8. To serve, cut in squares.

Sweet Lemon Bars

1 (14 ounce) can sweetened condensed milk	1(420 g)
½ cup lemon juice	125 ml
1½ teaspoons lemon zest or fresh lemon peel	7 ml
⅔ cup butter, softened	160 ml
1¼ cups packed light brown sugar	310 ml
1½ cups flour	375 ml
1 teaspoon baking powder	5 ml
¼ teaspoon salt	1 ml
1 cup oats	250 ml

1. Preheat oven to 350° (176° C).

2. In small bowl, mix condensed milk, lemon juice and lemon zest and set aside.

3. In mixing bowl, cream butter and brown sugar. Stir in flour, baking powder, salt and oats and mix until crumbly.

4. On bottom of greased 7 x 11-inch (18 x 28 cm) baking pan, press half crumbs and pour condensed milk mixture on top.

5. Sprinkle remaining crumb mixture over condensed milk and press down gently.

6. Bake at 350° (176° C) for 25 to 30 minutes or until bars brown slightly around edges.

7. Chill. Cut in bars to serve.

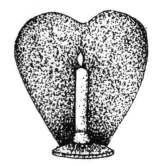

Lemon-Angel Bars

1 (16 ounce) package 1-step angel food cake mix	1 (454 g)
1 (20 ounce) can lemon pie filling	1 (570 g)
⅓ cup butter, softened	80 ml
2 cups powdered sugar	500 ml
2 tablespoons lemon juice	30 ml

1. Preheat oven to 350° (176° C).

2. In mixing bowl, combine cake mix and lemon pie filling and stir until it mixes well.

3. In greased, floured 9 x 13-inch (23 x 33 cm) baking pan, pour batter and bake 25 minutes.

4. Just before cake is done, combine butter, powdered sugar and lemon juice and spread over hot cake.

5. When cool, cut in bars. Store in refrigerator.

Lime Bars

2½ cups flour, divided	625 ml
1 cup powdered sugar, divided	250 ml
¾ cup (1½ sticks) butter	180 ml
4 eggs	4
2 cups sugar	500 ml
⅓ cup lime juice	80 ml
¾ teaspoon lime peel	4 ml
½ teaspoon baking powder	2 ml
1 lime, sliced for garnish	1

1. Preheat oven to 350° (176° C).

2. In bowl, combine 2 cups (500 ml) flour and ½ cup (125 ml) powdered sugar. Cut in butter until it resembles coarse crumbs.

3. Spoon into greased 9 x 13-inch (23 x 33 cm) baking dish and pat down with back of wooden spoon.

4. Bake for 15 to 20 minutes or until it begins to get light brown around edges.

5. In bowl, mix eggs, sugar, lime juice, lime peel and beat well. Combine baking powder and ½ cup (125 ml) remaining flour and whisk into egg-sugar mixture. Pour over hot crust.

6. Bake another 20 minutes or until just light brown. Cool.

7. Dust remaining powdered sugar with sifter and cut into squares. Place ⅛-inch (.5 cm) slice lime on each square.

Iced-Pineapple Squares

1½ cups sugar	375 ml
2 cups flour	500 ml
1½ teaspoons baking soda	7 ml
½ teaspoon salt	2 ml
1 (15 ounce) can crushed pineapple with juice	1 (438 g)
2 eggs	2

Frosting:

1½ cups sugar	375 ml
½ cup (1 stick) butter	125 ml
1 (5 ounce) can evaporated milk	1 (142 g)
1 cup chopped pecans	250 ml
1 (3½ ounce) can flaked coconut	1 (100 g)
1 teaspoon vanilla	5 ml

1. Preheat oven to 350° (176° C).

2. In mixing bowl, combine sugar, flour, baking soda, salt, pineapple and eggs and beat well.

3. In 9 x 13-inch (23 x 33 cm) greased, floured pan, pour batter and bake 35 minutes.

4. Prepare frosting as squares bake. In saucepan over medium heat, stir and mix sugar, butter and evaporated milk until mixture boils. Stir and boil 4 minutes.

5. Remove from heat and add pecans, coconut and vanilla. Spread frosting over hot squares. Serves 12.

Pumpkin-Pecan Squares

½ cup (1 stick) butter, softened	125 ml
1¼ cups packed brown sugar	310 ml
1½ cups flour	375 ml
1 cup oats	250 ml
1 teaspoon baking powder	5 ml
1 teaspoon salt, divided	5 ml
1 cup canned pumpkin	250 ml
1 (14 ounce) can sweetened condensed milk	1 (420 g)
2 eggs	2
¼ teaspoon cloves	1 ml
¼ teaspoon nutmeg	1 ml
½ teaspoon ginger	2 ml
1 teaspoon cinnamon	5 ml
1½ teaspoons vanilla	7 ml
1 cup chopped pecans	250 ml

1. Preheat oven to 350° (176° C).

2. In mixing bowl, beat butter, brown sugar, flour, oats, baking powder and ½ teaspoon (2 ml) salt and mix until mixture crumbles. Reserve ½ cup (125 ml) crumbled mixture.

3. In bottom of 10 x 15-inch (25 x 38 cm) greased baking pan, press remaining mixture and bake 20 minutes.

4. Using same mixing bowl, combine pumpkin, sweetened condensed milk, eggs, spices, vanilla and ½ teaspoon (2 ml) salt. Beat well and spread over crust. Bake 30 minutes.

5. Remove from oven. Combine reserved crumbled mixture and pecans and sprinkle over bars.

6. Return pan to oven and bake an additional 5 to 10 minutes.

7. Cool and cut in bars. Store covered in refrigerator.

Raspberry-Almond Squares

1½ cups flour	375 ml
½ cup sugar	125 ml
½ teaspoon baking powder	2 ml
½ teaspoon cinnamon	2 ml
½ cup (1 stick) butter, softened	125 ml
1 egg	1
½ teaspoon almond extract	2 ml
½ cup ground almonds	125 ml
1 (10 ounce) jar raspberry jam	1 (284 g)

Frosting:

½ cup powdered sugar	125 ml
2 teaspoons milk	10 ml
½ teaspoon almond extract	2 ml

1. Preheat oven to 350° (176° C).

2. In mixing bowl, combine flour, sugar, baking powder and cinnamon and gradually cut in butter.

3. Mix in egg, almond extract and almonds. Divide dough in half.

4. In greased, floured 9 x 9-inch (23 x 23 cm) baking pan, press half dough and spread with jam. Top with other half dough and press down gently.

5. Bake 35 to 40 minutes and cool.

6. To make frosting, combine powdered sugar, milk and almond extract in mixing bowl and stir until smooth. Drizzle over top.

7. Cut in squares to serve.

Raspberry-Crunch Bars

1¼ cups plus 2 tablespoons flour, divided	310 ml
⅔ cup sugar	160 ml
½ cup (1 stick) butter	125 ml
¾ cup raspberry jam	180 ml
3 eggs	3
⅔ cup packed light brown sugar	160 ml
1 teaspoon vanilla	5 ml
¼ teaspoon baking powder	1 ml
1¼ cups chopped pecans	310 ml

1. Preheat oven to 350° (176° C).

2. In bowl, combine 1¼ cups (310 ml) flour and sugar. Cut in butter until mixture is crumbly.

3. Press into buttered 9-inch (23 cm) baking pan and bake for 20 minutes or until edges are light brown. Spread raspberry jam over hot crust.

4. In mixing bowl, beat eggs, brown sugar, vanilla, remaining 2 tablespoons (30 ml) flour and baking powder. Stir just until well combined.

5. Stir in pecans. Spoon over jam and spread evenly.

6. Bake for another 18 minutes or until golden brown. Cool and cut into bars.

Raspberry-Shortbread Bars

1 (18 ounce) package butter cake mix	1 (520 g)
⅔ cup finely chopped pecans	160 ml
¼ cup (½ stick) butter, softened	60 ml
1 egg	1
1 (10 ounce) jar raspberry preserves	1 (284 g)

Frosting:

¾ cup powdered sugar	180 ml
1 tablespoon water	15 ml
½ teaspoon almond extract	2 ml

1. Preheat oven to 350° (176° C).

2. In mixing bowl with electric mixer, combine cake mix, pecans, butter and egg. Mix at low speed until mixture crumbles.

3. In bottom of greased, floured 9 x 13-inch (23 x 33 cm) baking pan, press mixture and spread with preserves.

4. Bake 25 minutes or until edges brown lightly. Cool.

5. In separate bowl, combine powdered sugar, water and almond extract and mix until smooth.

6. Drizzle frosting over warm shortbread.

7. Cut in bars to serve.

Strawberry Jam Bars

2 cups flour	500 ml
2 cups powdered sugar	500 ml
1 cup (2 sticks) butter, softened	250 ml
2 cups finely chopped pecans	500 ml
1⅓ cups strawberry preserves	330 ml

1. Preheat oven to 350° (176° C).

2. In mixing bowl, combine flour, sugar and butter and mix until crumbly.

3. Fold in pecans and set aside one third of this mixture.

4. In greased 9 x 13-inch (23 x 33 cm) baking dish, press remaining crumbly mixture.

5. Spread with preserves, sprinkle with remaining crumbly mixture and press lightly.

6. Bake 20 to 25 minutes or until tops brown lightly.

7. Cool completely before cutting in bars.

Absolutely Good Squares

Crust:

½ cup (1 stick) butter, softened	125 ml
⅓ cup sugar	80 ml
1 cup flour	250 ml

Filling:

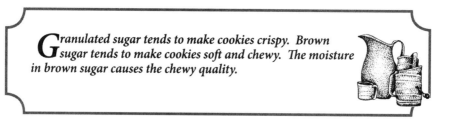

2 eggs, beaten	2
½ cup flaked coconut	125 ml
1⅔ cups brown sugar	410 ml
1½ cups macadamia nuts	375 ml
2 tablespoons flour	30 ml
2 teaspoons vanilla	10 ml
½ teaspoon baking powder	2 ml

1. Preheat oven to 350°(176° C).

2. In mixing bowl, combine butter, sugar and flour and mix well.

3. In bottom of 9-inch (23 cm) square pan, press dough and bake 20 minutes. (Crust does not need to brown.)

4. In large bowl, stir filling ingredients and mix well. Pour into hot baked crust.

5. Bake 20 to 25 minutes. Cool completely and cut into squares.

Granulated sugar tends to make cookies crispy. Brown sugar tends to make cookies soft and chewy. The moisture in brown sugar causes the chewy quality.

Brown Sugar Chews

1 cup packed brown sugar	250 ml
1 egg	1
1 teaspoon vanilla	5 ml
¼ teaspoon salt	1 ml
½ cup flour	125 ml
¼ teaspoon baking soda	1 ml
1 cup chopped pecans	250 ml
Sifted powdered sugar	

1. Preheat oven to 350° (176° C). Grease and flour 7 x 11-inch (18 x 28 cm) baking pan.

2. In mixing bowl with electric mixer, combine brown sugar, egg, vanilla, salt, flour and baking soda and beat until smooth. Add pecans and mix.

3. In baking dish, pour batter and bake 18 to 20 minutes. (Squares will be soft when removed from oven.) Cool.

4. Sprinkle sifted powdered sugar over chews. Cut in squares.

If you don't have brown sugar, add molasses to white sugar and mix. The more molasses you add, the darker the sugar.

Easy Cookie Bars

1 cup packed brown sugar	250 ml
½ cup sugar	125 ml
⅓ cup butter, softened	80 ml
1 egg	1
1 teaspoon vanilla	5 ml
1 teaspoon ground allspice	5 ml
1 teaspoon ground cinnamon	5 ml
2 cups buttermilk biscuit baking mix	500 ml
1 cup chopped pecans	250 ml

1. Preheat oven to 350° (176° C).

2. In mixing bowl, beat both sugars, butter, egg, vanilla, allspice and cinnamon and mix well. Add baking mix and stir well. Fold in pecans.

3. In ungreased 12 x 18-inch (30 x 46 cm) baking sheet with edges, spread batter evenly. (Batter may not quite cover pan completely, but will spread as it heats.) Bake 12 to 15 minutes.

4. Cut into bars immediately and remove from pan before completely cooled.

Bars are chewy when warm and crispy when cold.

There is no substitute for butter in baking. Margarine, light and whipped butter contain water and do not contain enough fat for baking.

Classic Pfeffernusse

½ cup (1 stick) butter, softened	125 ml
2/3 cup packed brown sugar	160 ml
1 egg	1
3 cups flour	750 ml
1 teaspoon cloves	5 ml
1 teaspoon ginger	5 ml
¾ teaspoon salt	4 ml
¼ teaspoon white pepper	1 ml
Powdered sugar	

1. Preheat oven to 325° (163° C). Blend butter, brown sugar and 1 egg.

2. In separate bowl, combine flour, cloves, ginger, salt and white pepper. Pour flour mixture into butter mixture and knead dough with hands until dough no longer sticks to hands.

3. Lightly flour board and pat dough out flat. Cut into small bars and place on greased cookie sheets.

4. Bake for about 15 minutes. Cool and roll in powdered sugar.

Cookie-Crunch Bars

1 (8 ounce) can crescent rolls	1 (228 g)
1 (14 ounce) can sweetened condensed milk	1 (420 g)
1 (16 ounce) package coconut-pecan icing mix	1 (454 g)
¼ cup (½ stick) butter, melted	60 ml

1. Preheat oven to 350° (176° C).

2. Spray sides of baking sheet with cooking spray and press crescent rolls together to cover baking sheet.

3. Bake 5 minutes and remove from oven. Pour sweetened condensed milk over rolls and spread evenly.

4. In medium bowl, combine icing mix and butter and sprinkle over sweetened condensed milk.

5. Bake 20 minutes or until crust browns.

6. When cool, cut in bars and store in refrigerator.

Rainbow Cookie Bars

½ cup (1 stick) butter	125 ml
2 cups graham cracker crumbs	500 ml
1 (14 ounce) can sweetened condensed milk	1 (420 g)
½ cup flaked coconut	125 ml
1 cup chopped pecans	250 ml
1 cup M&M candies	250 ml

1. Preheat oven to 350° (176° C).

2. In 9 x 13-inch (23 x 33 cm) baking pan, melt butter in oven.

3. Sprinkle crumbs over butter and pour condensed milk over crumbs.

4. Top with remaining ingredients and press down firmly.

5. Bake 25 to 30 minutes or until top browns lightly.

6. Cool and cut in bars.

Once when making these, I realized I was missing the M&M's, so I substituted white chocolate bits and they were great. The only thing lost was the rainbow.

Chewy Bars

3 eggs, beaten	3
1 (16 ounce) package light brown sugar	1 (454 g)
1 teaspoon vanilla	5 ml
½ cup (1 stick) butter, melted, slightly cooled	125 ml
2 cups flour	500 ml
2 teaspoons baking powder	10 ml
1½ cups chopped pecans	7 ml

1. Preheat oven to 350° (176° C).

2. In mixing bowl, combine eggs, brown sugar, vanilla and butter and mix well.

3. Gradually add flour and baking powder and mix well. Fold in pecans.

4. Grease and flour 9 x 13-inch (23 x 33 cm) baking pan and spread batter in pan.

5. Bake about 35 minutes. Bars are done when toothpick inserted in center comes out clean. If center is sticky, bake 4 to 5 minutes longer.

6. Cool and cut in squares.

Surprise Bars

1 (18 ounce) package yellow cake mix, divided	1 (520 g)
½ cup (1 stick) butter, melted	125 ml
4 eggs, divided	4
1 cup firmly packed brown sugar	250 ml
1½ cups corn syrup	375 ml
2 teaspoons vanilla	10 ml
1 cup chopped walnuts	250 ml

1. Preheat oven to 350° (176° C).

2. In bowl, combine one-third cake mix, melted butter and 1 egg and stir with fork until mixture crumbles. Set aside remaining cake mix.

3. In greased 9 x 13-inch (23 x 33 cm) baking pan, press batter and bake 15 minutes or just until top browns lightly.

4. In mixing bowl, combine remaining cake mix with remaining 3 eggs, brown sugar, corn syrup and vanilla. Beat on medium speed 2 minutes.

5. Pour over partially baked crust and sprinkle with walnuts.

6. Return to oven and bake another 30 to 35 minutes.

7. Cool and cut in bars.

Buttery Walnut Squares

Crust:

1 cup (2 sticks) butter, softened	250 ml
1¾ cups packed brown sugar	180 ml
1¾ cups flour	180 ml

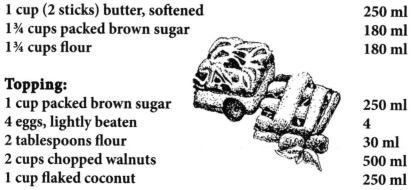

Topping:

1 cup packed brown sugar	250 ml
4 eggs, lightly beaten	4
2 tablespoons flour	30 ml
2 cups chopped walnuts	500 ml
1 cup flaked coconut	250 ml

1. Preheat oven to 350° (176° C).

2. In mixing bowl, cream butter and sugar. Add flour and mix well.

3. In greased 9 x 13-inch (23 x 33 cm) glass pan, pat mixture evenly and bake 15 minutes.

4. To make topping, combine sugar and eggs in medium bowl. Add flour and mix well.

5. Fold in walnuts and coconut and pour over crust.

6. Bake 20 to 25 minutes or just until center sets.

7. Cool in pan and cut in squares.

A scoop of ice cream really makes this a great dessert.

Brown Sugar Bars

1 cup flour	250 ml
2 teaspoons baking powder	10 ml
½ teaspoon salt	2 ml
1⅓ cups shortening	330 ml
2½ cups packed brown sugar	625 ml
2 eggs, beaten	2
2 teaspoons vanilla	10 ml
1½ cups chopped pecans	375 ml

1. Preheat oven to 350° (176° C).

2. In mixing bowl, combine flour, baking powder, salt, shortening, brown sugar and eggs. Beat slowly at first, then at higher speed until ingredients mix well.

3. Fold in vanilla and pecans and mix well.

4. In greased, floured 9 x 13-inch (23 x 33 cm) baking pan, spoon batter and bake 30 to 32 minutes. Cool and cut in bars to serve.

Crisco shortening was invented in 1911.

Love Those Bars

1 (18 ounce) box yellow cake mix	1 (520 g)
½ cup (1 stick) butter, softened	125 ml
3 eggs, divided	3
1 (6 ounce) package white chocolate chips	1 (170 g)
1 cup flaked coconut	250 ml
1 cup slivered almonds	250 ml
1 (16 ounce) box powdered sugar	1 (454 g)
1 (8 ounce) package cream cheese, softened	1 (228 g)

1. Preheat the over to 350° (176° C).

2. In mixing bowl, combine cake mix, butter and 2 eggs and beat well.

3. In bottom of lightly greased 9 x 13-inch (23 x 33 cm) baking pan, pat dough and top with layer of white chocolate chips.

4. Spread layer of coconut and layer of almonds on top and press gently with back of large spoon.

5. In separate bowl, combine powdered sugar, cream cheese and 1 egg and beat until creamy. Pour mixture over other ingredients.

6. Bake for 35 to 40 minutes.

7. Remove from oven and cool before cutting in bars.

Caramel Treats

1 cup (2 sticks) butter, softened   250 ml
1 (16 ounce) box dark brown sugar   1 (454 g)
2 eggs, beaten   2
1⅔ cups flour   410 ml
2 teaspoons baking powder   10 ml
⅛ teaspoon salt   .5 ml
2 teaspoons vanilla   10 ml
2 cups chopped pecans   500 ml
Powdered sugar

1. Preheat oven to 350° (176° C).

2. In large saucepan, combine butter and brown sugar and melt. Quickly remove from heat and cool.

3. Add eggs one at a time and beat well after each addition.

4. Add flour, baking powder, salt and vanilla and mix well. Stir in pecans.

5. In greased, floured 9 x 13-inch (23 x 33 cm) baking pan, pour batter and bake 25 to 30 minutes. Treats are done when toothpick inserted in center comes out clean.

6. Cool and dust with powdered sugar. Cut in squares.

*Be sure to use butter. There is no substitute
for the real thing in this recipe.*

Classic Carmelitas

Crust:

1 cup flour	250 ml
¾ cup packed brown sugar	180 ml
⅛ teaspoon salt	.5 ml
1 cup quick-cooking oats	250 ml
½ teaspoon baking soda	2 ml
¾ cup (1½ sticks) butter, melted	180 ml

Filling:

1 (6 ounce) package chocolate chips	1 (170 g)
¾ cup chopped pecans	180 ml
1 (12 ounce) jar caramel ice cream topping	1 (340 g)
3 tablespoons flour	45 ml
1 to 2 tablespoons water	15 to 30 ml

1. Preheat oven to 350° (176° C).

2. In mixing bowl with electric mixer, combine all crust ingredients and blend well to form crumbs.

3. Into greased 9 x 13-inch (23 x 33 cm) baking pan, press two-thirds crumb mixture and bake 10 minutes.

4. Remove from oven and sprinkle with chocolate chips and pecans.

5. In bowl, combine caramel topping, flour and water and spread over chips and pecans. Sprinkle with remaining crumb mixture.

6. Bake 20 minutes or until top turns golden brown. Chill 2 hours before cutting in squares.

Toffee Bars

1 cup (2 sticks) butter, softened	250 ml
1½ cups packed brown sugar	375 ml
1 egg	1
1 teaspoon vanilla	5 ml
2 cups flour	500 ml
¼ teaspoon salt	1 ml
2 cups chocolate chips	500 ml
½ cup finely chopped pecans	125 ml

1. Preheat oven to 350°(176° C).

2. In mixing bowl, cream butter, sugar, egg and vanilla and beat well.

3. Add flour and salt and stir to form smooth dough.

4. In greased, floured 9 x 13-inch (23 x 33 cm) baking pan, spread dough and bake 20 minutes.

5. Spread chocolate chips over bars as soon as pan is removed from oven.

6. When chocolate chips melt, spread chocolate over bars as frosting. Sprinkle pecans on top.

7. Cut in bars while still warm.

Heath bar and Skippy peanut butter were developed in 1932.

Puffy Cereal Bars

1 cup sugar	250 ml
1 cup light corn syrup	250 ml
1½ cups peanut butter	375 ml
6 cups puffed rice cereal	1.5 L
1 cup chocolate chips	250 ml
1 cup butterscotch chips	250 ml
½ cup chopped peanuts	125 ml

1. In saucepan, combine sugar and corn syrup, heat and stir until mixture boils.

2. Remove from heat and stir in peanut butter and cereal.

3. In greased, 9 x 13-inch (23 x 33 cm) baking dish, spread mixture evenly.

4. In saucepan over low heat, combine chocolate chips and butterscotch chips, heat and stir until chips melt.

5. Spread melted chips and peanuts over cereal layer. Chill until chips set.

6. Cut in bars and store in refrigerator.

*P*eter Pan peanut butter and Kellogg's *Rice Krispies were started in 1928.*

Classic Candied Gingerbread

1½ cups flour	375 ml
1 teaspoon baking soda	5 ml
1 teaspoon ground ginger	5 ml
1 teaspoon cinnamon	5 ml
½ cup (1 stick) butter, softened	125 ml
¾ cup firmly packed brown sugar	180 ml
2 eggs	2
¼ cup dark molasses	60 ml
⅔ cup buttermilk	160 ml
¼ cup finely chopped crystallized ginger	60 ml

1. Preheat oven to 350° (176° C). Grease and flour 8-inch or 9-inch (20 or 23 cm) square pan.

2. In medium bowl, sift flour, baking soda and spices and set aside.

3. In mixing bowl, beat butter until light and fluffy, then add sugar and beat again. Add eggs and beat well, then add molasses.

4. Stir half dry ingredients into butter mixture and beat. Add buttermilk and beat again. Add remaining ingredients and stir. Fold in crystallized ginger.

5. Pour batter in prepared pan and bake 45 minutes. Gingerbread is done when toothpick inserted in center comes out clean. Cut in squares and serve warm with butter.

Though the practice of baking gingerbread is centuries old, modern gingerbread may owe its popularity to the 19-century publication of the German fairy tale, Hansel and Gretel. Countries throughout Europe still bake traditional gingerbread houses, cakes and cookies. The popularity of gingerbread in America is especially evident at Christmastime, when children and adults alike participate in elaborate contests to see who can design the most breathtaking creation.

Gingerbread With Orange Sauce

½ cup shortening or butter, softened	125 ml
¾ cup sugar	180 ml
¾ cup molasses or syrup	180 ml
2 eggs	2
1 teaspoon baking soda	5 ml
½ cup buttermilk	125 ml
1 teaspoon ginger	5 ml
½ teaspoon cinnamon	2 ml
½ teaspoon nutmeg	2 ml
½ teaspoon ground cloves	2 ml
3½ cups flour	875 ml

1. Preheat oven to 350° (176° C). Blend butter, sugar and molasses until creamy. Fold in eggs, one at a time. Dissolve baking soda in buttermilk and pour into mixture. Mix well.

2. Combine ginger, cinnamon, nutmeg, cloves and flour in separate bowl and add gradually until mixture blends thoroughly. Pour into greased, floured 9 x 13-inch (23 x 33 cm) baking pan and bake for about 30 minutes.

Orange Sauce:
2 oranges
1 cup sugar
1 tablespoon butter

1. Squeeze 2 fresh oranges to get about ½ to ¾ cup freshly squeezed orange juice. Grate the rind (zest) to equal about 1 tablespoon and set aside.

2. Boil orange juice, sugar and butter just until sauce begins to thicken. Spoon over gingerbread while it is still hot and sprinkle orange zest over the top.

Old-Fashioned Cookies Index

C

E

F

L

Lemon
 Apricot Cookies 12
 Buttery Lemon Cookies 171
 Cream Cheese Cookies 134
 Ginger Gems 91
 Holiday Honey-Spice Cookies 190-191
 Lemon Cookies 66
 Lemon Drops 66
 Lemon Squares, Classic 246
 Lemonade Treats 64
 Lemon-Angel Bars 248
 Lemons On A Sugar Cloud 65
 Sweet Lemon Bars 247
Lemon Cookies 66
Lemon Drops 66
Lemon Squares, Classic 246
Lemonade Treats 64
Lemon-Angel Bars 248
Lemons On A Sugar Cloud 65
Lime Bars 249
Love Those Bars 266

M

Macadamia Crunchies 49
Macadamia Nut Bars 236
Macadamia Nut Cookies 50
Macadamia Nuts
 Absolutely Good Squares 256
 Macadamia Crunchies 49
 Macadamia Nut Bars 236
 Macadamia Nut Cookies 50
Magic Cookie Bars, Classic 210
Mairzy D' Oats 13
Maple Iced-Walnut Drops 9
Maraschino Cherubs 146
Melting Moments, Classic 97
Million Dollar Bars, Classic 224
Mincemeat Cookies, Classic 76
Marshmallows
 Chocolate Rocky Roads 216
 Chocolate-Marshmallow Squares 147
 Cobblestones 22
 Cocoa-Marshmallow Puffs 146
 Death By Chocolate 215
 Double-Dutch Pizza Cookie 177
 Jingle Bell Cookies 152
 Mairzy D' Oats 13
 No-Bake Cookies, Classic 138
 Rocky Road Bars, Classic 149
Mocha Chip Drops 8
Molasses Cookies, Classic 108

Monkey Faces 175
Monster Cookies 40
More Frostings For Cookies 174
Mother's Peanut Butter Cookies 52

N

No-Bake Cookies, Classic 138
None-Better Cookie 102
Nutty Butter Balls 158

O

Oats
 Apricot Squares 241
 Banana Cookies 60
 Banana-Oatmeal Cookies 123
 Best-Ever Cookies 44
 Buffalo Chip Cookies 136
 Butterscotch Crisp 88
 Butterscotch Meringues 89
 Caramel-Apple Squares 240
 Carmelitas, Classic 268
 Chewy Butterscotch Bars 223
 Chunky Oatmeal Bars 220
 Cocoa-Oatmeal Cookies 120
 Coconut Crunchies 79
 Coconut-Caramel Cookies 144
 Corn Flakes and Coconut Cookies 61
 Cowboy Cookies 45
 Crackerjack Cookies 126
 Fudge And Oat Bars 219
 Granny's Ginger Oat Cookies 118
 Hardy Carrot Cookies 10
 Mairzy D' Oats 13
 Oatmeal Crisps 122
 Oatmeal Sandwich Cookies, Classic 21
 Old-Fashioned Everyday
  Oatmeal Cookies 119
 Peanut Dream Bars, Classic 233
 Pumpkin-Pecan Squares 251
 Quick Oatmeal Cookies 142
 Raggedy Ann's, Classic 143
 Rhubarb Bars 234
 Shortbread Crunchies 94
 Snappy Oats 141
 Special K Cookies 127
 Spiced-Oatmeal Cookies 121
 Sweet Lemon Bars 247
 Texas Ranger Cookies 130
 Whippersnappers 137
 Wholesome Peanut Butter
  Cookies 188-189-189
 World's Best Bars 221
 World's Greatest Cookies 34

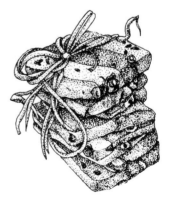

COOKBOOKS PUBLISHED BY COOKBOOK RESOURCES, LLC

The Ultimate Cooking with 4 Ingredients
Easy Cooking with 5 Ingredients
The Best of Cooking with 3 Ingredients
Gourmet Cooking with 5 Ingredients
Healthy Cooking with 4 Ingredients
Diabetic Cooking with 4 Ingredients
4-Ingredient Recipes for 30-Minute Meals
Essential 3-4-5 Ingredient Recipes
The Best 1001 Short, Easy Recipes
Easy Slow-Cooker Cookbook
Recipe Keeper
Quick Fixes with Cake Mixes
Casseroles to the Rescue
I Ain't On No Diet Cookbook
Kitchen Keepsakes/More Kitchen Keepsakes
Old-Fashioned Cookies
Grandmother's Cookies
Mother's Recipes
Recipe Keepsakes
Cookie Dough Secrets
Gifts for the Cookie Jar
All New Gifts for the Cookie Jar
Gifts in a Pickle Jar
Muffins In A Jar
Brownies In A Jar
Cookie Jar Magic
Easy Desserts
Bake Sale Bestsellers
Quilters' Cooking Companion
Miss Sadie's Southern Cooking
Classic Tex-Mex and Texas Cooking
Classic Southwest Cooking
The Great Canadian Cookbook
The Best of Lone Star Legacy Cookbook
Cookbook 25 Years
Pass the Plate
Texas Longhorn Cookbook
Trophy Hunters' Wild Game Cookbook
Mealtimes and Memories
Holiday Recipes
Little Taste of Texas
Little Taste of Texas II
Texas Peppers
Southwest Sizzler
Southwest Olé
Class Treats
Leaving Home

cookbook
resources LLC

To Order **Old-Fashioned Cookies**:

Please send_____ hard cover copies @ $19.95 (U.S.) each $_____

Texas residents add sales tax @ $1.60 each $_____

Please send_____ paperback copies @ $16.95 (U.S.) each $_____

Texas residents add sales tax @ $1.34 each $_____

Plus postage/handling @ $6.00 each $_____

$1.00 (each additional copy) $_____

Check or Credit Card (Canada-credit card only) **Total** $_____

Charge to my ❑ [MasterCard] or ❑ [VISA]

Account #_____

Expiration Date_____

Signature_____

Mail or Call:
Cookbook Resources
541 Doubletree Dr.
Highland Village, Texas 75077
Toll Free (866) 229-2665
(972) 317-6404 Fax

Name_____

Address_____

City_____State_____Zip_____

Phone (day)_____(night)_____

Phone (day)_____(night)_____

To Order **Old-Fashioned Cookies**:

Please send_____ hard cover copies @ $19.95 (U.S.) each $_____

Texas residents add sales tax @ $1.60 each $_____

Please send_____ paperback copies @ $16.95 (U.S.) each $_____

Texas residents add sales tax @ $1.34 each $_____

Plus postage/handling @ $6.00 each $_____

$1.00 (each additional copy) $_____

Check or Credit Card (Canada-credit card only) **Total** $_____

Charge to my ❑ [MasterCard] or ❑ [VISA]

Account #_____

Expiration Date_____

Signature_____

Mail or Call:
Cookbook Resources
541 Doubletree Dr.
Highland Village, Texas 75077
Toll Free (866) 229-2665
(972) 317-6404 Fax

Name_____

Address_____

City_____State_____Zip_____

Phone (day)_____(night)_____

Phone (day)_____(night)_____